Get Set for Psychology

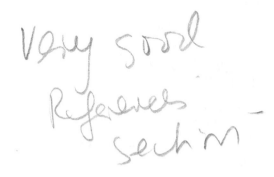

Get Set for Psychology

Peter Wright and Hamish Macleod

Edinburgh University Press

© Peter Wright and Hamish Macleod, 2006

Edinburgh University Press Ltd
22 George Square, Edinburgh

Typeset in Sabon
by Servis Filmsetting Ltd, Manchester, and
printed and bound in Great Britain by
Antony Rowe Ltd, Chippenham, Wilts

A CIP record for this book is available from the British Library

ISBN-10 0 7486 2096 6 (paperback)
ISBN-13 978 0 7486 2096 8 (paperback)

CONTENTS

PART I: UNDERSTANDING PSYCHOLOGY

PART II: THE UNIVERSITY EXPERIENCE AND PSYCHOLOGY

PART I
Understanding Psychology

1 HOW TO USE THIS BOOK

This book is about starting to study psychology at university. Before we begin, however, we would like to say a little bit about what we are trying to do in the book. We believe that many learning experiences are less successful than they could be because the people involved do not share a common understanding of what it is that is supposed to be happening, and about just what the intended outcomes might be. This is a theme that we will return to elsewhere in the book in relation to your future studies. But we would like to say something here about what the book is, and is not. It is *not* an introduction to the subject of psychology. There are many excellent introductory texts, and we are not seeking to compete with these. We have not set out to give a comprehensive overview of the subject, but rather to explore one or two typical examples of the concerns of academic psychology, and to give an impression of the ways in which psychologists think and talk about human behaviour and experience. Similarly, there are lots of good 'study guides' that will provide valuable advice about how to address the array of tasks with which you will be faced at university. This book tries to give you a general orientation towards your studies.

The book is divided into two parts – the psychology part and the studying part. We would like to encourage you from the start, however, to link the two areas in your mind as much as you can. There are two reasons for this; one quite general and the other very specific. First of all the general point – one that might be made by any university teacher writing a book about studying in his or her subject area. The ways in which different subjects are studied depends to some extent on the nature of the subject. Let us put it like this: studying psychology at university is more about <u>becoming a psychologist than</u>

it is about remembering lots of facts about psychology. People who research the business of higher education talk about 'ways of thinking and practising in the discipline'. What goes on at the surface – the lectures, the tutorials, visits to the library – will be very similar from one subject to the next, but the underlying methods and habits of thought may be quite different. For example, psychology and history are both subjects that depend heavily on the evaluation of evidence and the construction of arguments about how things are. However, what counts as evidence, or the ways in which arguments are formed, will be subtly different.

Now the more specific point. The academic discipline of psychology concerns itself with matters of:

- comprehension
- memory
- learning
- social groups
- collaboration
- competition

That is, the very things which are central to living and working at a university. If you are studying psychology you simply must take advantage of these concerns, by reflecting on your own experiences of work and learning. All students can benefit from a reflective approach to their learning and study, but a student of psychology has the advantage of studying the very things that will help him or her to do this.

Again, let us consider this from two angles. First of all, your own experiences, and those of the people around you, will serve as valuable subject matter for your thinking about psychology. Observe what goes on around you, and let these observations inform your thinking about human behaviour. Don't let this get out of hand, however!

Further, what you discover about human learning, thought, problem solving and attention will help you to work and study more effectively. What you learn about communication, hierarchy and group processes will help you to understand what is going on – from an interpersonal point of view – in the lecture room, tutorial class or student union bar.

We will try to extend some of these threads from time to time in what follows.

CHOOSING YOUR DEGREE PROGRAMME

Aside from academic considerations there are many factors that will help you to choose the university at which you want to study. Perhaps you want to be as close to (or far from) your home as you can possibly manage. It may be that the institution is located in a particularly beautiful or vibrant city, or that a group of you from school have resolved to go up to university together – wherever that happens to be. And if you have no particular reason to choose one institution over another on academic grounds, these non-academic reasons may be perfectly satisfactory bases for a decision. There are, however, a few academic issues that you might want to consider before you fall back on entirely social and aesthetic criteria.

It is important to realise that an undergraduate degree in psychology will not qualify you to practice as a psychologist – in education, for example, or as a clinical or sports psychologist. You may have noticed, when you look at either websites or prospectuses for psychology at different universities, that the degree programme is accredited by the British Psychological Society (BPS). This is an important proviso if you wish to undertake a career as a professional psychologist. An accredited degree is one for which the programme of teaching across the final two years (in the case of an English University) or the final three years (in the case of the four-year Scottish Honours degree) is considered a thorough training in specified areas of psychology. If you obtain a minimum 2:2 Honours degree on an accredited programme you are eligible to become a graduate member of the society, and eventually after acceptance onto a suitable postgraduate training course, register as a Chartered Psychologist. This is a statement to the public at large that you are recognised as a practitioner by the BPS, similar to other professional qualifications in medicine and nursing, for example. There are now many training courses in addition to the three mentioned above – educational, clinical and sports psychology – including those in health, forensic and counselling psychology. All involve several years of study and the completion of a piece of original research. Whereas almost all universities in the UK will offer undergraduate courses in psychology, postgraduate training courses are more dispersed.

THE BRITISH PSYCHOLOGICAL SOCIETY

The BPS is an excellent membership organisation and you should, during your undergraduate years, give serious consideration to becoming one of its student subscribers. That completion of a degree programme conveys the basis of graduate membership of the BPS is, however, much less important for many people than they might at first think. In our own institution (Edinburgh), perhaps as few as 10–15 per cent of graduates go on to further study towards a professional qualification in psychology. The degree in psychology constitutes an excellent general education, and can lead on to many areas of professional employment not directly related to psychology. The skills you will acquire in your degree (IT skills in running experiments and managing data; the manipulation of data-sets using statistical packages; the design and execution of original research projects; the communication skills acquired in testing volunteers or presenting papers in seminars; the evaluation of scientific evidence in support of two opposing views) all are recognised by employers as a substantial undergraduate training. Psychology combines both the critical and experimental skills of the scientist and fosters the creative thinking said to be more characteristic of the arts graduate.

Even for those students who realise the broader benefits of studying psychology, BPS accreditation of their course keeps open a number of important career options that they would be ill-advised to throw away at the outset. You would have to be very sure that professional qualification as a psychologist was not on your career agenda before you entered an undergraduate programme which was not BPS accredited. If this is important to you, make sure that you find out whether the degree programmes for which you plan to apply are so accredited, and look at the website of the BPS (www.bps.org.uk). As a psychology undergraduate you are able to become a student member of the society and attend meetings and conferences, and participate in the lively student section. With membership comes a monthly copy of *The Psychologist* with news, views, articles and current events of interest to psychologists. In addition you can register for an electronic research digest, which will regularly inform you of new developments in different fields.

DIFFERENT KINDS OF PSYCHOLOGY DEGREES

There are many excellent degree programmes in the social sciences which do not carry BPS accreditation. This is not because they lack anything in academic quality, but rather that they combine studies in psychology with a range of other subject areas, and thus do not contain enough psychology to satisfy the accreditation requirements of the BPS. The very attraction of these programmes may be their wide variety of cover, and so some applicants will find them appropriate. However, if you decide that such a broad social sciences programme is for you, then subsequently find yourself attracted to a career in psychology, all is not lost. A number of institutions now offer 'conversion' courses (usually one year full-time or two years part-time) that will allow you to 'upgrade' your qualification. But in this, as in other things, it is better to plan ahead.

The general coverage of any undergraduate programme in psychology that carries BPS accreditation will be very similar. If your interests in the subject are very general, you cannot go far wrong. There are, however, some reasons why you might want to do a bit of preliminary research on programmes and departments in which they are taught before you apply. First of all, the opportunities to study particular specialist options may vary greatly from institution to institution. For example, the psychology department in our own institution has a prominent team researching in parapsychology (the study of anomalous or paranormal experiences and abilities), while it does not, at the time of writing, offer any options in forensic or sports psychology. The internet makes it an easy matter to find out about a teaching department and explore the variety of topics that it researches and teaches. If you believe that your interests in psychology are at present quite general, you might find that particular enthusiasms will be awakened by doing the rounds of a few university websites, looking at the range of research interests of the teaching and research staff. Be aware, however, that just because an institution carries out research in a particular area of interest, it does not mean that this will be represented in its undergraduate teaching. If in any doubt, ask.

This brings us to a second reason why you might want to find out more about a university's psychology department before you apply to study there: to learn something about the people who will be teaching you. For some people there is great excitement in knowing that those who are teaching them about language acquisition, for example, or the brain bases of mental disorders, are not only teaching the topic, but are in the forefront of researching and defining what that topic is now, and will be in the future. While there is no guarantee that great researchers will also be great teachers (we will return later to the different styles and approaches that you are likely to encounter among university teachers), enthusiasm can be inspiring and infectious. It is impossible to make clear recommendations in matters like this, as it will be very much a question of personal taste.

How do you make decisions like this? You are trying to find a setting that will suit you; one into which you feel that you will fit. For example, in some universities the psychology programmes are taught alongside the sciences, particularly the biological sciences. Elsewhere they may be taught alongside the social sciences (like sociology or social anthropology), or with philosophy or mathematics. Considerations like this may help you find somewhere that you feel 'at home'.

STUDYING PSYCHOLOGY BEFORE UNIVERSITY

In 1990 about 9,000 students obtained passes in A level psychology; by 2005 this figure was in excess of 50,000. In the first year of AS awards there were 48,342 made in psychology; this rose to over 75,000 in 2005. When psychology at Higher level was introduced in Scotland in 2000, there were 300 passes; within two years this number had increased fivefold. In short, the introduction of psychology in schools as a pre-university subject has excited huge interest with an exponential growth in numbers of students. The BPS produced a report in 2003 examining this growth in post-16 qualifications, and enquiring as to the implications for university degree courses. As yet there is little evidence that pre-university qualifications are taken into account when designing first year psychology courses. The assumption is that the subject should be taught from scratch, and there is no systematic evidence that we are aware of on whether a prior qualification in psychology has any bearing on student performance in the first year of a degree course. The BPS report includes the views of students who had A level qualifications, and it is interesting to note that despite their syllabus covering the five core areas of psychology – cognition and biological, social, developmental and individual differences – many students were surprised at how scientific the university course was. This reflects the view that psychologists have of their discipline – it is a science. Inevitably this means that the teaching and acquisition of good skills in the design, execution and evaluation of the data resulting from psychology experiments is paramount (see Chapter 3). So if you do have a psychology background when you start your degree, you will have a clear advantage compared to those without such a background in terms of your familiarity with basic concepts and the approach of psychology. You may find a good deal of your first year course is familiar, but as your lecturers are likely to be qualified psychologists – not often the case in schools – there will be a different emphasis in the teaching, and an expectation for you to be familiar with the evidence base of the topics taught rather than accepting everything as read.

REFERENCES

As this book is intended both for those students as yet uncertain about choosing psychology as their major subject area and for those about to start such a degree, we have provided very few references drawn from scholarly academic journals, since these are only available through specialist libraries. You will encounter such journals once you get to university, and an essential part of your training will be to evaluate evidence from the primary source material. Here you will find at the end of each chapter a list of some popular books in that area, which you should be able to find either in your local library or in bookshops. We also list articles drawn from *The Psychologist* which, although covering up-to-date material, are written in a way that does not assume extensive background knowledge. Articles from January 1998 are all available online from the BPS website, and can be downloaded as well as read from the screen. Go to the BPS website at www.bps.org.uk and click on 'The Psychologist' from the 'Quick Links' menu; then click on 'Search The Psychologist Online' and find the volume and article you want to view. By clicking on the title you can download this as a PDF document. You will need Adobe Acrobat Reader installed on your machine to view this. The articles are an extension of material you will find in the chapters, and by using the site you will almost certainly come across plenty of other readings which will be of interest.

FURTHER READING

Gregory, L. Richard (2004, 2nd edition), *Oxford Companion to the Mind*, Oxford: Oxford University Press.
As a reviewer in *The Psychologist* wrote, this is a perfect present for any psychologist or would-be psychology student. Unlike most encyclopaedia-style books, this is a readable mine of information for your degree years and beyond. The editor, Richard Gregory, is the ideal guide for a grand tour of the mind; engaging and personable, his stamp is impressed

throughout with humour, insights and eccentricity. There are some 900 articles on every aspect of the brain and conscious-ness and over 300 contributors from the world's leading scholars.

Sternberg, J. Robert (2003, 4th edition), *The Psychologist's Companion,* Cambridge: Cambridge University Press.
Although intended for graduate students and beyond, this book will make easy reading for the psychology student looking for a comprehensive guide on all aspects of writing during a degree programme. It covers a wealth of topics, including misconceptions about psychology papers, steps in writing library research papers and experimental research papers, rules for writing psychology papers, commonly misused words, internet resources, guidelines for data presen-tation, references for psychology papers and standards for evaluating psychology papers.

2 STATISTICAL THINKING

As a 'science of behaviour', psychology is about tendencies and not absolutes. One cannot say that when certain circumstances are true, a particular behaviour will inevitably occur, but rather that the probability of that behaviour occurring will be increased. For example, we may say that men are more likely to behave aggressively than women in certain circumstances, but that is not to say that we will not encounter some particularly aggressive women and some admirably restrained men. Or perhaps we want to claim that anxiety will lead to poorer performance in an exam situation, yet for some individuals a mild degree of anxiety may be just the spur that they need to perform better. What we are saying, then, is that generalisations can be helpful, but they are not always going to be correct when one considers any individual case.

Psychological research is therefore highly dependent on that branch of mathematics known as statistics in making sense of its findings. If you study psychology at university you will almost certainly have to take a course in statistics at some point, or you may find that some element of statistics will be included in each year of your study.

It is fair to say that statistics is not a popular topic among undergraduate psychologists, and many would try to avoid it if they could. Likewise attitudes towards statistics are far from clear among teaching staff. While course descriptions will emphasise the importance of statistics, individual teachers may not appear concerned about, or aware of, the 'details' of certain statistical approaches, and it will often be the most junior members of a department who will be given the task of teaching the area.

There is a paradox here, and we would not wish to offer any simple explanations. But we would like to suggest that the paradox could be understood to a certain extent by distinguishing between two senses in which statistics can be seen as important to the study of psychology:

- as a set of tools for handling research data;
- as a way of thinking about the nature of research evidence.

Having made this distinction, we have to confess straight away that it is an artificial one. It is most likely the case, for example, that an understanding of the second (thinking about evidence) comes through learning about and working with the first (applying statistical procedures to research data). Many students, however, get no further than the first, seeing statistics as about 'doing the calculations', and fail to engage in a useful and meaningful way with the second. That is, until they come to work on their own research, when they may well develop a new understanding of statistics as an aid to communicating the meaning of some piece of evidence that they feel particularly involved with and enthusiastic about. On the other hand, some of your teachers may have so internalised the business of thinking statistically that they have forgotten much of what they once knew about the details of conducting a particular calculation, and thus are less than clear when they try to communicate an understanding to you. We hope that this is not your experience.

In this chapter we are going to try to convince you about the importance and power of statistical thinking, leaving aside any mathematical detail. We will do this by describing a number of research problems in psychology that can only be fully explored and discussed by using ideas from statistics and probability. If we succeed, we know that you will be able to develop competence in these tools when the time comes.

There are really two reasons why you will need, as a student of psychology, to develop your statistical awareness. The first is obvious. You will be asked to carry out research, interpret the results and communicate your findings to others. The second is equally important, and arguably more important in the longer term. You need to be able to understand and evaluate the claims of others. You may come across these claims in the published psychological literature during your undergraduate days, and you should always work very hard to ask yourself, 'Do these claims follow from this evidence, or might there be another explanation?'. But you will also find claims in political speeches, government reports, commercial advertising and news items which your studies as a psychologist, and a well-developed statistical awareness, will help you to evaluate sceptically. Whatever you hear, you should always be prepared to believe but inclined to question.

A WORD ABOUT COMPUTERS

Few people actually do the sums of statistical calculations themselves anymore, but rather use some statistical analysis 'package' (a suite of programs) on a computer. This is fine, but you still have to learn enough to know what analysis to carry out and how to interpret what the computer gives you at the end. The other point to remember is that the computer will almost certainly manage to give you some kind of answer, even if the analysis that you asked for was inappropriate. Don't go to the computer too quickly. Learn to 'eyeball' your data, and get a feel for the patterns that it contains. This will come with experience.

STATISTICAL TERMINOLOGY

Coming to grips with statistical thinking can be difficult because of the range of technical words that are used. Even worse, these words are often common ones that are used in this context in very particular ways – since they are common we are sometimes seduced into thinking that we understand what is being meant when in fact we don't. Words like 'normal', 'error', 'variable', 'significance' and 'relationship' all have very specific meanings in the context of statistical thinking. But that is just the way language works. We frequently call on words to do double duty. The word 'sheet', for example, might have a very different meaning if you were talking to a yacht skipper or a nurse.

Measurement

Measurement in psychology appears to be a difficult notion for some people, and quasi-moral objections are voiced about 'reducing human experience to numbers'. Quantification, however, is best understood as a particular use of language to describe behaviour and experience, which serves certain purposes. For example, it is particularly useful for comparing things. A poet might describe himself as 'lonely as a cloud'[1], or another 'as low and lonely as the rain'[2]. They are clearly talking about a psychological state, and the use of language has a certain power and purpose. But it is not a scientific purpose. It does not make sense, for example, to ask if 'cloud' is lonelier than 'rain' – although you may have views about that. Measurement enables us to get a certain sort of handle on things, and much of the skill in conducting psychological research is about finding good ways to measure the qualities that we are interested in. This endeavour need not be seen as any assault on the value or uniqueness of human experience.

Levels of Measurement

One of the simplest measurements that we could make would be the presence or absence of something. Do you have, or are you now working towards, a pre-university qualification in psychology? The answer to that question is either yes or no. Asking that question is an act of measurement, and your answer is a measurement that is a characteristic (albeit a very

---

[1] From 'I Wandered Lonely as a Cloud', by William Wordsworth.
[2] From 'As the Rain', by Jeb Loy Nichols.

minor one) of you. That is really all there is to it – the rest is detail.

Another question would be to ask just what qualification you have, or are working towards. In the UK, the possibilities might be the Scottish Higher Grade, or the A Level, as well as some others. If you live outside the UK there would be other responses that you could give. To ask whether or not, or to ask what, in this context, would be described as a nominal measurement. Think of nominal measurement as 'naming' something, or putting something into a category.

Let's stay with the business of psychology qualifications, but move on a bit. We might ask someone what was the highest level to which they had studied psychology. The possible answers might be 'not at all'; 'at school'; 'introductory level at university or college'; 'an undergraduate degree'; 'a postgraduate degree'. You will see that these possible answers are arranged in an order that corresponds roughly to the amount of psychology that we might expect the person to know. This would be described as an ordinal measurement, as the possible answers can be placed in *order* of the level of formal qualification.

Many studies in experimental psychology depend on how quickly a person can react to a question or a stimulus, or on how many mistakes they make in a number of trials of a simple task. Reaction times, or error rates, would be examples of yet another sort of measurement called an interval measurement. An interval scale is one in which equal divisions on the scale correspond to equal amounts of something. Interval measurement is probably the sort of measurement with which you are most familiar. When you measure someone's height in centimetres, or their age in years, this would be an example of interval measurement.

Variables

Let's take the word 'variable' now. We use it here as a noun rather than an adjective, so 'variables' is not a misprint.

A variable is something that can vary. Think of it as an attribute that can vary from person to person, or from situation to situation. Experience tells us that we already have the potential to confuse variable with measurement. The variable is the attribute being measured, and the measurement is the value taken by the variable for any given individual and situation. Let us say that we are interested in eye colour. Eye colour is a variable that can take a number of values (brown, blue, green, grey). The measured values of the variable eye colour for the authors of this book are blue (HM) and brown (PW).

Correlation

Psychologists are often interested in being able to predict one thing from another. From what we know of this person, are they likely to be a successful army officer? If this convicted criminal is released on parole, are they likely to reoffend? Is a driver's reaction to a traffic emergency slowed by the consumption of alcohol? Is there a relationship between stress and heart disease? These are all questions about correlation, or the way in which two or more variables change together. Some of the questions are much simpler than others, and a phrase like 'what we know about this person' hides the vast complexity of psychological measurement. But psychologists are often involved in finding good means of measuring 'aptitude' in ways that will help employers predict who would be good at a particular job.

A straightforward example of correlation can be shown in the relationship between task complexity and time taken to complete it. Try a small experiment on yourself. Take a pack of playing cards and set aside the jokers. Hold the pack face up, and deal all the cards into two piles. Time how long this task takes you. Next, take the pack again and, holding the cards face up, sort them into two piles of either black or red cards. How long did this take? In the same way, sort the pack into four piles according to suit (clubs, spades, hearts and diamonds). How long? You should find that the more complex the task, the longer it takes. There is a correlation between task complexity and time to complete.

Correlation and Causation

In the above card sorting example, it is pretty clear that the increased task complexity causes you to slow down. Similarly, if we find that there is a correlation between daily ice cream sales at a seaside café and the average daily temperature, we would feel fairly confident in suggesting that hot weather made people buy more ice cream, rather than believing that increasing ice cream sales caused the temperature to rise. In these examples we use correlation to infer causation.

The understanding of psychological relationships, however, is rarely that simple. Let us suggest that we find young people convicted for crimes of violence to be more likely than the general population to spend time playing violent video games. Do we conclude that the game-playing experience has been a stimulus to the violent acts for which these people have been convicted? Some have argued precisely this. We might, alternatively, want to consider the possibility that people prone to acts of violence will be differentially likely to select the playing of violent video games as a pastime. We must be careful not to jump too quickly to the conclusion that when A and B are correlated, then variations in A cause variations in B. It may be that the direction of causation is quite the reverse, or even that A and B are actually independent of one another, and the correlation that we find is actually due to them both being influenced by some third variable of which we are completely unaware.

Error

We commonly think of the word 'error' as meaning 'a mistake'. We make an error in a calculation, and we get the wrong answer. The term 'error' in a statistical context, however, refers to the accuracy with which we are able to make a measurement. This use of the word occurs in a phrase like 'margin of error'. This notion is important when it comes to making judgements about how confident we feel we can be in drawing conclusions from our research.

Significance

This is another word with a common meaning that is subtly different from its technical meaning in statistical terms. A news item might speak of 'a significant breakthrough in AIDS research', and we would understand this to mean that some important discovery or advance had been made. A significant finding in statistical terms, however, means simply one that is better than might be expected by chance alone. Significance in this sense is a key concept in the understanding of data analysis.

Experiments

An experiment is an approach to answering the question 'What is the effect of X on Y?'. For example, what is the effect of environmental noise on the accuracy of carrying out a skilled task? What is the effect of hunger on taste sensitivity? What is the effect of studying with the TV on, on the retention of the information being studied?

An experiment represents an attempt to control certain aspects of a situation while allowing others to vary in systematic ways. This systematic variation is sometimes referred to as manipulation. In the simplest case, an experiment involves the manipulation of one variable and the measurement of another, while holding all other aspects of the situation constant. The jargon here is that the variable we manipulate is called the independent variable, while the variable we measure is referred to as the dependent variable.

Changes in the dependent variable *depend* on the manipulations we make in the independent variable.

Let's consider a particular example here. Studies have been carried out to look at the way in which the mind uses mental images in its decision-making processes, using the time taken to respond to questions as an index of the difficulty of the task. If you were asked to visualise a dog, and were then asked whether a dog had legs, it would take less time (on average – remember the notion of 'error' discussed above) to confirm this than it would take you to confirm that the dog had claws. That is, the more particular the detail, the longer the question takes to answer. It is as if you held a picture of a dog in your mind, and had to 'look more closely' to answer the question about claws as compared with the question about legs. In this study, the dependent variable is the time taken to respond to the question. Perhaps you are given two buttons, labelled 'yes' and 'no', and the exact time taken to press either button can be recorded. The independent variable will be the level of detail addressed in the question. In this example, two levels of detail are mentioned.

Selecting and Assigning Participants

Let's say that you are interested in the effectiveness of a particular educational approach with primary school children. Perhaps there is a certain literacy scheme that you believe will lead to more rapid, confident and lasting reading and writing development. How might you go about evaluating this approach? There are a number of problems that make this a very tricky proposition indeed. Logically, you could find two classes of children who are at identical stages in literacy development, leave one class alone, and introduce your new literacy scheme to the other. If your new literacy scheme is what you believe it to be, then the class using it will show a more rapid development than the others. We can slip in some more terminology here: the group of pupils working with the new literacy scheme will be said to be the experimental group (or in the experimental condition), and the group working with the traditional approach will be the control group (or in the control condition).

Pause for a moment before you read on, and see how many problems you can think of with this naive model.

First, there is an ethical difficulty. What if you are right, and this literacy scheme will really improve learning in the experimental group? Is it acceptable to deny that advantage to the other children? What if you are wrong, and the novel approach does really bad things to the children's grasp of reading? How would you feel then? There are a number of ways to address these concerns, which mostly amount to abandoning the notion of a control group. You might work with all the children, monitoring their progress with the traditional approach for a period, then introducing the new approach and monitoring their progress again. You would then need to show that the rate of literacy improvement was greater during the experimental period than during the control period. This, of course, introduces other problems. What if the children improve more quickly with the new scheme? Does that mean the new scheme is better? Not necessarily. It might just be that novelty is good.

We could describe this general class of difficulty as a matter of order effects. It is not that the two conditions are different with respect to the children's cognitive performance, but rather that change in itself acts as a stimulation to the children's motivation. We could address this (perhaps) by monitoring the children for three periods rather than two, returning after the period of working with the new scheme to a final period working with the traditional scheme again. If it is really the scheme itself that is making the difference, we would expect the pace of development to take a downturn when we return to the traditional approach. But, again, is that the correct inference? Perhaps there is something about the experience of working with the new scheme that makes it difficult for the children to return to the original approach; this would be described as a negative transfer effect. It is not that the traditional approach is poor, rather that the experience of the new approach disrupts its effectiveness when the children go back to working with it. And so it goes on. We can address one problem, but introduce a few more new ones.

There are also some further logistic problems that might arise. We suggested above that the two groups of children would have to be 'identical'. If they were not starting in the same place with respect to reading ability, how can one reasonably make comparisons between the two groups at the end of the study? But what are the chances of finding two classes at just the same level of development like this? Pretty slim. We can get around this one by working with subsets of the children rather than the whole class. As far as possible, we find a child in one class who is matched (on the relevant dimensions like ability, educational achievement and probably age and gender as well for good measure) with a child in the other class. Instead of comparing two whole classes, we compare a series of matched pairs. We simply leave out, for the purposes of the analysis of our results, the children who we are not able to match. Statistically speaking, this is quite a powerful approach, and we may choose it even if it is not dictated by the organisational circumstances.

You might be hoping that we will logically work our way through this morass of methodological difficulties, finally to arrive at the Right Way. Unfortunately, this is rarely the case. In laboratory studies concerned with reaction times, memory for word lists, sensory acuity or sentence comprehension we may be able to set up a nicely balanced experimental design, with control groups and all possible order effects addressed, but in the real world it is seldom possible, and compromises have to be made.

Naturalistic Experiments

One way around such ethical concerns is to abandon the notion of experimental manipulation and rather to look for naturally occurring variance to work with. Pursuing the above example, perhaps two schools decide independently to work with two different literacy schemes. You might monitor the success of the children under the two regimes. The decision to innovate, or to stay with the traditional approach, does not lie with you, and has been taken for other good and grounded reasons. Or perhaps you want to study the impact of some aspect of family background on drug abuse. You would gather background information from a group of drug users and a matched group of non-users (although defining what you mean by 'matched' is in itself a complex question), and look for the effects predicted by your theory. Naturalistic experiments are sometimes called correlational experiments. We have talked already about the difficulty of inferring causation from correlation, and this problem always exists in such naturalistic studies.

Wider Applicability of Research

Like the idea of measurement, the notion of experiment can cause difficulties for some people. The situation of unnatural control which the experimental method implies is held by some to mean that little of importance can be learned from it about normal and naturally occurring human behaviour and experience. Here we might be inclined to compare the conventional sense of the word 'significant' with its meaning when applied statistically. Perhaps the results of an experimental study can be shown to be statistically significant, and yet the significance (in the sense of importance or worth) of the findings would be questioned on the grounds that the circumstances in which the data were collected were unnatural. Questions can therefore be asked about just how widely the results can be generalised, and used to predict outcomes in other settings.

CONCLUSION

This chapter has had a lot to say about the difficulties of doing psychological research. There are often no easy or correct answers to the question of how to design successful studies that give you information about the matters in which you are interested. Research design is often a case of finding a compromise between the important imperatives of theoretical rigour, practical and logistical possibilities and ethical responsibilities. Understanding the competing demands is crucial to the business of designing and conducting research, and of evaluating the research activities of others.

FURTHER READING

Boyle, David (2001), *The Tyranny of Numbers: Why Counting Can't Make Us Happy*, London: HarperCollins.
An entertaining polemic which questions the scientific obsession with measurement. It should be taken with a large dose of salt, but nevertheless is an interesting and absorbing read.

Clark-Carter, David, et al. (2003), Special issue on statistics, *The Psychologist*, vol. 12, December 2003, pp. 631–48.
An excellent series of papers dealing with new developments in statistics. Although much of it may seem too advanced for the beginning student, there are useful discussions on how computer software adds power to statistical thinking, why we should be using a particular sample size in our experimental designs, and how best to report and present data graphically.

3 PRACTICAL CLASSES

Is psychology a science? This is a common debate, and it would be unusual for someone to complete an undergraduate degree in psychology without having discussed this topic in a tutorial, or without having been faced with some variant of the question in an examination paper. The answer is, of course, by no means clear. The historical roots of psychology are located in the philosophy of the mind, and in experimental physiology of sensations, and it has gone through phases in which the preferred methods of the day have ranged from the observation of external behaviours to introspection – personal reflection on one's own internal mental states. It is therefore very difficult to give a definitive historical answer to the question. There is, however, one clear sense in which psychology, as taught in undergraduate programmes in the UK, can be said to be a science. That is, like physics, chemistry, biology or other subjects that one can easily identify as being sciences, the programme will always contain an element of 'laboratory work' in the timetable. In that respect at least psychology is unlike those other subjects traditionally regarded as humanities or social sciences.

If you are coming from secondary school with an experience of 'science' subjects you will be familiar with the conduct of the 'lab class' or the 'practical', but if your background has been in 'arts' subjects this may be something that you have never come across before. Whatever your background, however you should not feel too anxious, or too complacent. Practical classes in psychology are an area to which everyone has strengths to bring, and everyone finds particular learning challenges.

WHY PRACTICALS?

However subtle the question of psychology's status as a science, there is a tradition in many areas of psychology of operating within a framework of hypothesis and experimentation. Put simply, our understanding of the subject has progressed by the formulation of ideas about how things are, followed by the construction of situations in which those ideas can be put to the test. This is the essence of experimental design, and the skills involved in the testing of hypotheses are an important aspect of what it is to be a psychologist. Furthermore, these are vital transferable skills that are valued and sought after in the world of employment. Evaluating the relative success of a range of advertising campaigns, improving the interface of a piece of computer software or gathering attitudes on behalf of a charity would all be activities that psychology practical classes will prepare you for.

THE PRACTICAL CLASS ENVIRONMENT

The tasks you may be set in a psychology practical class can be extremely varied. We will continue to use the term 'practical class' here, as only some of the exercises you will carry out will take place in anything one might recognise as a 'laboratory'. You might be sent out onto the campus to gather information from your student colleagues, or to observe some aspect of people's behaviour in public places. Some useful studies can be carried out at home, with the participation of your friends, based on very simple materials like lists of words to be remembered, or playing cards to be sorted in various ways. It is the nature of psychology that important phenomena can be powerfully demonstrated with very simple techniques.

Here is an example. You can try this out on yourself, and you will almost certainly find that the effect shows up. It will show itself more strongly, however, if the participant doesn't know what is expected. We talk of participants in psychological research as being naive about the predicted outcome, and this is often critically important if we want to claim that the results that we obtain have not been influenced by the participants' expectations. These matters of setting up and running experiments (experimental design) are discussed further in Chapter 2. Here is your task. Below are two lists. The lists are made up of either one, two, three or four characters. Go down each list – List 1 followed by List 2 – saying aloud the number of characters on each line of the list, but ignoring entirely the actual characters themselves.

List 1

H F H

F

F F H F

F H

H H

F H F

H F

F F F H

H

F

List 2

4

2

1 1 1 1

4 4

2 2 2

3 3

1 1

3 3 3 3

2

4 4 4

How did you get on? You can stop reading now, if you like, and think about what you experienced in carrying out this task.

What we expect you experienced was that it was harder to read the second list than the first list. You probably had to read more slowly, and found yourself stumbling over the business of reading aloud two fours as 'two' rather than 'four'. You were told to ignore the actual characters, and to read only the number of each printed on the line, but you were unable to do so. The irrelevant information (or information that was arbitrarily declared to be irrelevant in the experiment) intruded into your conduct of the task. When the task was to count the number of items there was no intrusion when these items were alphabetic characters, but there was intrusion when the characters themselves were numbers.

Try this experiment out on a few of your friends or family members. It would probably be best to copy the lists onto the middle of separate sheets of paper. It would also make the effect show more clearly if you doubled the lengths of the lists. Think of this experiment in the context of Chapter 2, on statistical thinking. Here are some questions for you about how you might improve the design of what we have presented to you as a very crude 'it worked / it didn't work' demonstration.

- What might you measure and record in this experiment?

- What sources of bias might exist, and how might you seek to eliminate them?

- What additional conditions might you want to add to the above two (conflict / no conflict)?

WHAT YOU WILL BE LEARNING

There are a number of reasons why the designers of under-graduate psychology programmes put an element of practical work into their courses. One reason is that such practical work is required to be present in any programme that is accredited by the British Psychological Society. For the reasons described above, practical work is held by the BPS to be a defining aspect of an undergraduate psychology degree, and an essential part of any programme that they will accredit as the basis for membership of the society and for further professional training in psychology.

The practical class will be your opportunity to learn about the conduct of research in psychology. You will learn how to design and to carry out various sorts of studies, including experiments, surveys, observational studies and various forms of qualitative research. Understanding how research is designed and carried out will not only help you to collect your own data in your senior years as a student, or in some work setting after your graduation, but will also help you to understand the limitations of published research that you read about, and to judge the value of its findings.

Designing your study and gathering data will only be the beginning, of course. The data will have to be analysed, and your findings communicated to others. The analysis of data we have already talked about a little in Chapter 2. Communication and dissemination are key aspects of the research process. An important skill that you will learn in the context of the practical class will be the writing of a research report, and we will say a little more about this later. You may be asked to communicate your findings in other ways, such as a poster illustrating your study or the delivery of a brief oral presentation. The written report, the poster and the oral presentation are all traditional ways by which the findings of research are communicated to the wider academic community. The practical class is an important opportunity for the student to begin to develop as a junior member of that community. Although it does not happen often, we have certainly had experiences of seeing research carried out by students in the first through to the final years of their studies being presented as posters or oral presentations at academic conferences.

ETHICS IN PSYCHOLOGICAL RESEARCH

A vital aspect of carrying out research in psychology is working with the people who will help you by participating in your studies. To get the best out of people you have to treat them with respect and courtesy. You have to communicate clearly to them what you want them to do, anticipating any misunderstandings that might arise. There are, of course, important ethical considerations to be kept in mind when carrying out research with human participants. People have a right to know what they are letting themselves in for, and to withdraw from the study if anything seems unacceptable to them. It would be wrong, for example, to tell participants that a task would take up five minutes of their time when you know that it is more likely to take half an hour. Yet this notion of informed consent has to be balanced against the need to keep the participants naive about certain aspects of the study. It would clearly not be acceptable to do anything that causes your participants significant distress or anxiety. What is 'significant' in this context is a matter of judgement. It might be acceptable, for instance, to introduce a 'surprise' memory test that participants had not been anticipating, but it would not be acceptable to 'surprise' them in a way that caused genuine fright. If you wanted to surprise people in that sense of the word (perhaps to look at some physiological consequence of the fright response, such as increased heart rate), you would have to inform them about your intentions and about the range of stimuli that they might experience (sudden noises, mild electric shocks or the lights going out) and obtain their agreement to continue, making it clear to them that they could withdraw from the experiment at any time.

Important too would be the debriefing of your participants. We often find out a lot about psychological mechanisms by seeing how those mechanisms 'break down' under certain sorts of pressure. Think about the example experiment we described above; we learn something about unconscious processing of irrelevant information by looking at the errors that people make when conflict exists. If there were not stumblings and errors then the task was too simple, and we learn nothing. Errors are good, in other words. But we must remember that our participants almost inevitably think of experiments as 'tests', and want to perform well in them. What pleases us (a nice error rate) will distress them. We must show sensitivity to this, and reassure them at the end of the study about how well they have done, why certain aspects of the task felt difficult and why the difficulties that they have experienced have also been experienced by all the other participants. In general, then, there are important social skills that can be practised and developed in the context of the practical class.

ACTIVE LEARNING

The practical class may often be used as an adjunct to the lecture programme on your course. The lectures may set out a theoretical area for you to think about, and the practical class will provide an opportunity for some of the associated phenomena to be demonstrated and explored. For example, you might be discussing perceptual systems in your lectures while carrying out experiments in the practical class to map the sensitivity of different regions of the eye. Or you might be hearing about attitude change in the lectures and exploring in a practical how different sorts of persuasive message might contribute to more or less movement in expressed attitudes. In short, the practical class is an excellent opportunity to engage in active learning. The ancient Chinese philosopher Confucius is reputed to have observed:

I hear – I forget
I see – I remember
I do – I understand

Practical classes are very good opportunities to do things that will help your understanding of the topics you are studying.

Having said this, there can be complexities in matching up the theoretical and the practical, and you should not always expect the links between practical classes and lectures to be exact and obvious. First of all, there may be a mismatch for logistic reasons. Lectures may have to be moved around in the programme across the year because of the availability of the people who are presenting them, while it may be less easy to move one practical class because it depends on you having certain statistical knowledge, or on the availability of some technical resources. You should try to be sensitive to these constraints, and make what linkages you can. Furthermore, the theoretical links that you should be making are perhaps not the most obvious and superficial ones. For example, you may be carrying out a study in word recall, which is placed at that particular point in the course because of the complexity of the statistical analysis that it requires rather than being *primarily* designed to relate to your course on memory – although it will do that as well. Your teachers will help you to make these sorts of links, and you should discuss such issues with them.

YOUR TEACHERS

This would be a good point to mention the importance of the practical classes as an opportunity to discuss your work with your teachers. A practical class may often be timetabled for about three hours in the week. As we indicated above, not all of this time will be spent in a classroom setting. In addition, these classes will usually be quite busy times, in which planning and organisation on your part will be necessary to get through the work. On some occasions, however, there will be 'slack time', while you are waiting for something else to happen. This time provides a chance to have useful conversations with your senior colleagues.

Teachers in practical classes are sometimes referred to as demonstrators. The demonstrators may be members of the lecturing staff in your department, or they may be research students working on psychological or related projects. Having a research student as your demonstrator should not be seen as an inferior situation. Since they will be developing their own research skills at the time, they may be more sensitive to the difficulties that you are having with research methodology and statistics. If, on the other hand, your demonstrator happens to be a member of the lecturing staff, they may have a wider overview of the course and be in a position to do more to help you to make a wide range of theoretical links with your practical work. The practical class tends to be quite a 'social event' with a large group of undergraduates working with three or more demonstrators, each with different strengths, skills and expertise. When the mix works well it can be an extremely stimulating and enjoyable experience for all involved.

The other people you will encounter in and around practical classes will the technical and research support staff of your department. These people are employed for their skills in electronics, computing or video production, or some other area of expertise that they bring to the support of teaching and research in the department. While these colleagues will not direct research projects themselves, or be involved with the planning of the teaching, they are often highly experienced in the simple business of getting things to work. They will not have formal teaching responsibilities, but are nonetheless people from whom you will learn a great deal. And their importance to you will increase as you come to design and conduct your own individual research studies in your senior years.

FIELDWORK

Fieldwork is the term usually applied to research activity which takes place away from the laboratory or classroom. This term is more commonly used in subjects like ecology or botany, where one may be literally carrying out one's research on a hillside or seashore. You may experience fieldwork of this sort in a psychology programme with a significant component of animal behaviour in the curriculum, when you may find yourself visiting sea cliffs to watch the nesting behaviour of seagulls, or a farmyard to make observations on the behaviour of domestic animals. The term is also be applied, however, to situations in which you are asked to make observations of human behaviour in a naturalistic setting. Fieldwork in this sense might take you into a supermarket to observe the behaviour of people in checkout queues, into a library or museum to gather information about how people search for information or into a school playground to watch children playing together.

DOING REAL EXPERIMENTS

With all respect to our colleagues in the physical and biological sciences, there is a sense in which we would like to offer psychology, as experienced in the early undergraduate years, as a better exposure to the essence of the scientific method than many other subjects more usually regarded as examples of sciences. In these other scientific areas it is often necessary for students to learn the methods and techniques of scientific investigation by carrying out a series of pre-defined experiments, the expected results of which are certainly known by the teachers, and perhaps even by the students themselves, before the experiment is carried out. While there are certainly experiments of this sort in introductory psychology courses, it is possible for students to progress very quickly to a situation in which they can ask questions, and design and carry out studies to address those questions, where the answers cannot be predicted beforehand with any degree of certainty by themselves or their teachers. Thus students are able to feel the 'thrill of the chase' in a way which is very close to the experience of a research scientist.

WRITING A RESEARCH REPORT

Writing a report on a piece of work is the frequent culmination of a practical class exercise, and represents an important communicative skill. The report should outline where the ideas for the research have come from, describe the research that was carried out, present and describe the findings and discuss any conclusions that can be drawn. Research reports are usually rigorously assessed, so you will normally be given clear guidelines about their format which you should be careful to follow. Poster or oral presentations should cover the same ground as a full written report, but may contain less detail. The general pattern of what needs to be included is described below.

Like a good essay, a good research report will begin with a title that describes what the study is about. Ideally, the title will convey something of the question that the research has addressed for example:

The effect of caffeine on reaction time in a visual search task.

Memory for abstract and concrete words, using a visualisation mnemonic technique.

Preferences for sweet and savoury tastes in fed and fasting human subjects.

An introductory section will describe where the ideas for the research have come. This is likely to be a summary of the recent published literature on the topic, indicating how the present research will extend, or challenge, earlier work. A methods section will follow, describing just how the research was carried out. A good way to think about this section is to include any information that would be needed by another person who came along and wanted to repeat your research exactly as you had done it. It should describe the number and particular characteristics of the people who participated in your study (the participants). It is important to mention how they were recruited, their age and gender, and any other features important to the study. This section also describes what equipment you used, and what was done (your procedure). Equipment might be some paper and a pencil, a computer or some other piece of research apparatus. An important aspect of the description of your procedure would be a verbatim record of any instructions that you gave your participants. The results section will set out your findings in a clear and accessible way. If your data are quantitative, then tables or graphs may be the best way to communicate them. Some techniques for statistical analysis have already been discussed in Chapter 2. Finally, the report would have a discussion section which draws together how you believe your results should be understood, and what they mean. In this section you might return to the earlier published literature on the topic, relating it to what you have found and highlighting important areas of agreement or disagreement. A good piece of research will raise as many questions as it answers, and the discussion section can usefully close with suggestions for further research that needs to follow from what you have discovered and observed.

The writing of a research report for a psychology practical class is a great deal like many real-world tasks that you will be set in your employment after graduation. The ability to communicate your conclusions clearly from the evidence gathered, and to present a persuasive argument in favour of a certain future course of action, are skills that will be valuable in many work settings.

CONCLUSION

Practical classes are excellent opportunities for active learning of the theoretical aspects of your course. A good practical class should also be a highly motivating experience, as it is in the process of learning about and carrying out research studies of your own that you come closest to the experience of 'becoming a psychologist', which is so important to your personal and intellectual development.

FURTHER READING

Dunbar, George (2005), *Evaluating Research Methods in Psychology: A Case Study Approach*, Oxford: Blackwell. Using a series of more than forty case studies, this text illustrates the processes and pitfalls involved in evaluating psychological research. The author describes each case in a clear and concise manner, and then invites the reader to consider whether the conclusion drawn at the end of the case is correct or whether the results could have an alternative explanation. The cases reflect the range of research methods taught at undergraduate level and include qualitative research. This case-study approach should help you appreciate the difficulties of designing research, whether your own or that of others.

4   BIOLOGICAL BASES OF BEHAVIOUR

There are a number of related areas of psychology that concern themselves with what might be described as the biological bases of human behaviour and experience. Some psychology students are surprised at the amount of biology they are expected to know, and it is worth emphasising that we are both social and biological beings. Any consideration of the social relations between individuals is impoverished if it neglects the underlying biology, in the same way as an extreme reductionist view of human behaviour which considers only biological mechanisms. It is of course possible to specialise in different areas of psychology, but an understanding of basic biological processes is a strong prerequisite for most psychological explanations.

THE HUMAN BRAIN

The brain is a rather unprepossessing organ. There is nothing in its gross physical appearance to suggest just what it might be for. It has a highly convoluted surface, rather like a large, soft walnut, and weighs on average just over a Kilogram. Early anatomists thought that it might be a system for cooling the blood which is, as it happens, something that the brain does extremely well – those who engage in outdoor sports will know how much heat we lose through our heads. The function of many other organs is clear from their physical appearance and from what they are connected to: the heart pumps blood, for instance, and the stomach and intestines clearly have something to do with the ingestion and processing of food. As a result of the effects of brain damage in accident or combat injury it gradually came to be realised that the brain had something to do with mind and experience. Even then, it was thought for some time that it was not the outer tissue of the brain that was important but rather the fluid-filled cavities (the ventricles) in the centre. We now know that the pressure of fluid in the ventricles helps to provide structural support to the weight of nervous tissue inside the skull.

Early in the nineteenth century Franz-Joseph Gall (and subsequently his protégé Johann Kaspar Spurzheim) argued that the brain was the organ of the mind, and that the surface of the brain was composed of a number of different faculties or propensities – the extent of which could be measured by palpating the surface of the head. This idea became known as phrenology and proved extremely popular for more than fifty years. It is an interesting example of how a correct idea emerges but the evidence on which it is based is entirely spurious. The phrenologists were right in emphasising, for the first time, that it was possible to localise function to different regions of the cerebral cortex (the superficial and most evolved region of the brain), but failed to develop rigorous methods to verify this. They were entirely incorrect, however, in believing that the surface of the skull bore any necessary relation to the underlying brain tissue. Rather than attempt to correlate surface features with particular behaviour, Gall was extremely predisposed to see a cranial prominence (a high-domed forehead) when he already had evidence of a striking behaviour (a person of exceptional memory or high intelligence). The use of appropriate control procedures and statistical methods, which are the norm today, would have quickly shown that there was no basis to the phrenologists' views.

In the latter half of the nineteenth century, individual case histories finally established that different psychological functions and behaviour were related to different regions of the brain. Two particularly striking examples are those of Phineas Gage and, in the twentieth century, the patient known as H. M.

Phineas Gage was a roadworker in North America who blasted rockfaces apart during road construction. He suffered an unfortunate accident in which the three-foot iron rod, which he used to pack down gunpowder in the rock, slipped from his hand, igniting the powder and blowing the rod through the front part of his skull. The injury, which destroyed much of his frontal lobes, resulted in a profound alteration of his personality. He changed from being a quiet, moderate and religious man to a loud-mouthed, profane and libidinous character.

H. M. is probably the most famous patient in neurological history, following his surgery for the relief of intractable epilepsy. The operation involved the removal of both temporal lobes (the portion of the cerebral cortex which lies on the side of the head roughly below and above the position of the ears) and underlying parts of the phylogenetically older components of the brain (that is, in evolutionary terms), in particular the region known as the hippocampus. This surgery, while improving his epilepsy, left H. M. with a profound loss of memory of all events that followed his operation. His memory of his life before the surgery was unaffected, but the subsequent fifty years were a complete blank to him as he was unable to form any new long-term memories.

50 first dates film

NERVE CELLS

The tissue of the brain, like that of the rest of the body, is made up of many individual cells. There are two principal types of cells in the brain, nerve cells and glial cells. Nerve cells (or neurons) carry out the processing which is the basis of human thought and experience, while the current thinking about glial cells is that they serve to support and nourish nerve cells. There is not the scope here to describe the nature of nerve cells, save to say that what chiefly characterises them is that there are lots of them and that they are connected together in often highly complex ways. The 'lots' in this instance comes to about one hundred billion. The neuroscientist Susan Greenfield has provided a powerful way of thinking about this number by estimating that there are approximately the same number of trees in the Amazon rainforest as individual nerve cells in each of our brains. She further suggests that the number of connections between the nerve cells in our brains would closely approximate the number of leaves on all those trees. This provides for a system of truly staggering complexity.

The complexity of the brain has been a source of excitement for those who have studied it and attempted to understand its workings. The neurophysiologist Sir Charles Sherrington, for instance, described the brain as 'an enchanted loom, where millions of flashing shuttles weave a dissolving pattern', his lyrical description conveying something of this wonder and excitement. Although we now know very much more about the workings of the brain than we did when Sherrington was working in this early part of the twentieth century, the wonder and excitement still remains for those working in this area. And it is clear that brain science also holds a fascination for the general public, as it seems to be concerned with the exploration of what makes us what we are.

Nerve Cell Connections

Most people know that the conduction of information along nerve cells is an electrical process, and that this electrical activity produces tiny signals which can be detected by sensors on the surface of the skull – the so-called electroencephalograph. When nerves connect to one another, however, the signal that passes between them is in all but a few cases not a direct electrical event, but rather is a chemical process. The point at which one nerve cell connects to the next is called the synapse. At the synapse there is a tiny gap between the cells, and the arrival of an electrical signal triggers the release of a chemical from the surface of the first cell that moves across the gap to have its effect on the second cell. This chemical is called a transmitter substance. It is at the synapse that the individual 'decisions' of nerve cell interaction are made. If there is sufficient transmitter substance, which usually means that several pre-synaptic cells have been active at once or in quick succession, the post-synaptic nerve cell will take up the signal and pass it on.

When we learn something new and this information is stored as a memory of the event this must produce a change somewhere in the nervous system. Contemporary research indicates this is almost certainly a change in the ease or difficulty with which one nerve cell influences another at the synapse. The ability of the synapse to alter its efficacy is known as plasticity, and there is enormous interest in this property. Research into nerve cell connection often involves a collaboration between neuroscientists and psychologists, since inevitably such experiments may involve examining these biological changes which occur as an animal or a human learns a new task. You will not be required to carry out such experiments as part of your undergraduate training, but you will be expected to understand the logic behind them, and the problems in interpreting such work.

CHEMICAL SYSTEMS IN THE BRAIN

Discussion of synapses, and the chemical molecules in the minute spaces between individual nerve cells, may seem like a level of detail far removed from the concerns of human behaviour and experience. However, it is because of the similarity of their shape to the naturally occurring transmitters that drugs such as LSD or mescaline have their profound mind-altering effects. An example of this would be the body's natural response to pain, and the analgesic (pain-reducing) action of morphine and other related drugs. Pain is a protective mechanism designed to make us favour an injured part so that no more damage is done and so that the injury has time to heal. There are times, however, when it is better for us in the long run to ignore pain – in a fight situation, for example, or when the thing that has injured us might feel inclined to carry on eating us. In those cases, the brain releases chemicals that serve to damp down our response to pain. These chemicals have come to be known as endorphins, which is short for endogenous morphines. The word 'endogenous' simply means 'originating internally'. Endorphins keep soldiers functioning when they are injured in battle, and explain remarkable accounts of footballers playing out games with severe injuries that would incapacitate them were they not competitively aroused. They also explain the so called 'jogger's high' experienced by some athletes in intense training. The molecule of the drug morphine has a shape that is similar to these naturally occurring pain control chemicals, and so has the ability to reduce pain by acting on the receptor sites in the brain normally triggered by these natural substances.

How Nerves Signal Information

When a nerve cell is active it is said to 'fire'. Either a nerve fires, or it does not. There is no gradation in the intensity of an individual nerve's response. It is said to be an 'all-or-none' system. If the nervous system wants to signal the intensity of something it does it through the rate at which the nerve cell fires. Let's consider something simple like the intensity of a light falling on the eye. As light intensity increases, the rate of nerve firing increases, and as the intensity decreases the firing rate falls again. Let's consider a more complicated stimulus situation. Imagine that you are sitting in a moving train, looking out of the window. The countryside is passing by, and you are conscious of a continuous stream of movement. The train pulls into a station and stops. You are conscious that the train appears to be drifting backwards. But when you fix a particular point on the station building with the edge of the window, you realise that nothing is moving. Perhaps you have never noticed this illusion. Look out for it the next time you travel on a train or bus. It is an example of a motion after-effect. Another classic example of this is the Waterfall Illusion. Find a waterfall of your choice, and stare at the water pouring downwards for a few minutes. Then transfer your gaze quickly to a fixed point on the bank, like a rock or a plant. The object at which you look will appear to drift slowly upwards. The nervous system responds maximally when things change, and when a stimulus is constant for some time the rate of firing of the nerve cells decreases. The visual system in the brain has cells that respond to motion, and when there is a constant stream of motion across the eye their rate of firing will decrease. They are said to adapt. Hence the disparity in the firing of cells which respond to movement in opposite directions provides the illusion of movement in the opposite direction.

Images of the Brain

An important area of brain science today concerns the ways that have been developed to enable us to view images of the brain and, more importantly, to do this in near real-time in a conscious and mentally active experimental participant. These techniques, collectively described as functional brain imaging, enable us to gain information about which areas of the brain are most active under particular circumstances of sensory experience or mental activity. As nerve cells become more active in firing, they require more energy brought to them as nutrients and oxygen in the blood supply. Changes in the blood supply to particular regions of the brain produce slight differences in temperature. These differences can be picked up and produce a picture of the brain – usually coloured such that red regions indicate increased activity.

Here is one example of this kind of research. We described earlier that the brain injury of the patient H. M. who suffered from severe memory problems, included a region known as the hippocampus. A particular theory about the functions of the hippocampus gives it a very unique connection with spatial memory, and animal experiments indicate that if the hippocampus is damaged or inactive then learning which is dependent on understanding the spatial relationships between objects in the environment becomes impossible. If volunteers are asked to play a computer game which involves finding their way around a virtual environment, this region of the brain is shown to be more active in one form of brain imaging known as fMRI (functional Magnetic Resonance Imaging). Further evidence of the importance of this relationship is the demonstration that those London taxi drivers who possess the 'knowledge' (the nickname for an intimate familiarity with the map of London and all the quickest routes) have particular regions of the hippocampus which have increased in volume. This is an excellent example of the idea of plasticity referred to earlier – in this case an increase in the amount of nerve tissue with a specialised function as the result of a particular experience.

THE ROLE OF HORMONES

A second communication system within the body is that of the endocrine or hormone glands – ductless glands that secrete chemicals into the bloodstream and cause effects at a site remote from where they are produced. One of the first hormones to be described was insulin, which is produced by the pancreas and which regulates blood glucose levels. Many of these hormones have very direct influences on behaviour – for example, testosterone and oestrogen, the male and female hormones. The presence of secondary sexual characteristics, such as the brightly coloured comb of the cockerel or the antlers of the deer, are a direct measure of the amount of testosterone present in the blood and can be used as an assay (test) for the hormone. Hormones can play a role both in the expression of a particular behaviour and in the development of the brain to permit the expression of that behaviour when adult. In mammals there is good evidence that the basic brain design is that of the female (the default brain); only if the male hormone testosterone is present at a critical period in early development will the brain become masculinised and allow appropriate gender specific behaviour when adult.

Some hormones follow a seasonal or cyclical pattern. This is, of course, true for the human menstrual cycle, in which for women who have reached puberty there is a rise and fall of both oestrogen and progesterone at different phases of the cycle. The highest levels of oestrogen occur at mid-cycle when a women is most fertile. This peak of oestrogen affects sensory acuity, and in recent experiments results in males judging females to be more attractive at this stage (an interesting example to think about in connection with evolutionary approaches). The sharp fall in oestrogen and the rise of progesterone which occurs in the later phase of the cycle can produce the negative mood swings and irritability associated with premenstrual tension.

COMPARATIVE PSYCHOLOGY

Much research in behavioural science concerns the behaviour and mental abilities of non-human animals. Some of this research is carried out by zoologists and ecologists interested in the lives and habits of the animals that they study. Some is directed towards concern for animal welfare in agricultural settings, to understand how farm animals can be housed in humane and minimally stressful conditions. Studies of animal behaviour can also contribute significantly to our understanding of human psychology, and this is the field of work called comparative psychology. Comparisons between humans and other animals frequently reveal that similar behavioural problems are often addressed in very similar ways across the animal kingdom. However, some of the most important findings from studies of animal behaviour are those that show that even apparently closely related species can address and solve behavioural problems in interestingly different ways which are well suited to the environments in which they live.

EVOLUTIONARY PSYCHOLOGY

Charles Darwin's theory of evolution by natural selection has been highly influential in modern biology. Variations in physical characteristics arise in the general population as a result of spontaneous mutations of the genetic bases of these characteristics. If a characteristic enhances the individual's fitness (defined as their likelihood of surviving and reproducing), then the incidence of this characteristic will increase in the population. Thus some changes are lost, while others are retained and increase in frequency. Furthermore, this new characteristic may not be of any practical value at all, but simply increases the individual's chances of attracting a mate and successfully reproducing. The classic example of this would be the massive tail of the peacock which, although it slows the individual down and increases the chance that it will be caught by a predator, has been selected by evolution because it plays a key role in the mating displays of the bird. But why on earth *should* this ridiculous tail be found to be attractive by peahens? One very convincing argument, often referred to as the Handicap Principal, is that the very fact that an individual peacock has survived with this massive appendage must mean that he has the Right Stuff in other important respects to peahens.

Evolutionary psychology is based simply on the argument that if selection mechanisms have brought about the physical characteristics of plants and animals, they must also underlie behavioural and psychological mechanisms. (Darwin, indeed, wrote quite a bit on the behaviour of plants, but we need not go into that here.) That is, we can consider any aspect of the operation of the human mind and ask 'What was this designed for?' or 'Why does this convey an evolutionary advantage?'

This is a very powerful approach to thinking about human behaviour, and can potentially provide insights in any area of psychological endeavour. It is an increasingly popular approach, with many books being published on the topic. Yet it is an approach that can also spark intense controversy, often apparently based on what detractors seem to believe that it should imply rather than what is actually being claimed. There is a traditional, though fundamentally flawed, discussion in psychology which is known as the nature/nurture debate. Briefly stated, the discussion is about how much of our behaviour or psychological characteristics are attributable to our inherited background ('nature') and how much to the experiences that we have ('nurture'). This, however, is a misleading way to think of these issues; a better approach is to suggest that our fundamental human nature ultimately displays itself through the experiences that we have in our lives. Human nature shows itself to be highly varied, but it is not found to be infinitely malleable. It might be said that a child can grow

up to speak any language depending on the language spoken
to it by its care-givers. But rather we should say that the child
can acquire any *human* language. We can imagine many forms
of alien language, based for example on a system of skin pig-
mentation like that of the octopus, or the whistling of dolphins
or the electrical discharges of the electric eel. A human child
would not be able to learn the language of a small furry crea-
ture from Alpha Centauri.

FURTHER READING

Carter, R. (1998), *Mapping the Mind*, London: Phoenix.
Rita Carter is a medical writer who regularly contributes to
the *New Scientist* and the *Independent*. *Mapping the Mind*
charts the way human behaviour and culture have been
moulded by the landscape of the brain. Carter shows how our
personalities reflect the biological mechanisms underlying
thought and emotion, and how behavioural eccentricities may
be traced to abnormalities in the individual brain.

Greenfield, S. (1997), *The Human Brain: A Guided Tour*
     London: Phoenix.
Susan Greenfield is professor of pharmacology at Oxford
University and became director of the Royal Institution of
Great Britain in 1998. In 1994 she was the first woman to
give the Royal Institution's Christmas lectures, and has sub-
sequently made a wide range of broadcasts on TV and radio,
including regular appearances on The BBC's *Tomorrow's
World* and *Breakfast TV*.

Special issue on evolutionary psychology, *The Psychologist*,
     vol. 14, August 2001, pp. 414–31.
Special issue on 3,4-methylenedioxymethamphetamine
     (MDMA), commonly known as ecstasy, *The Psychologist*,
     vol. 15, September 2002, pp. 464–74.
Both these issues are examples of a much used format in aca-
demic journals. A leading authority is asked to write a key

target article which is then distributed to a group of academic peers for comment. The target article and the peer commentary are published together with the original authors' response to the commentaries. This enables the reader to see where the strengths and weaknesses of the argument seem to lie, and, of course, how far their own criticisms agree with of the authors'.

Ridley, M. (2004), *Nature Via Nurture: Genes, Experience and What Makes Us Human*, London: Harper Perennial. Matt Ridley did research in zoology at Oxford before becoming a journalist. He worked for *The Economist* for eight years and has been a columnist for both the *Sunday Telegraph* and the *Daily Telegraph*. In this book he argues that nurture depends on genes, while genes also need nurture. Genes not only predetermine the broad structure of the brain, they also absorb formative experiences, react to social cues and even run memory.

Plasticity?.

5 PERCEPTION

The study of perception concerns us with the question of how we come to know things about the world around us. The word derives from the Latin *percipere*, meaning to seize or understand. This is one of the areas in which psychology comes very close to philosophy, as philosophy also involves thinking about the nature of knowledge, and with how it is that objects and events in the outside world can come to have an influence on the mind.

The traditional debate regarding perception was between empiricism, which held that all we know about the world is learned through the medium of our senses, and nativism, which held that we all arrive in the world with a certain amount of innate knowledge. For the empiricists, the mind of the infant was a *tabula rasa* (literally, a blank slate), upon which experience imprinted itself. The problem that the nativists tried to address was just how a system that did not already know anything would be able to make any sense of the information that it encountered in the world. To cut an extremely long story short, it couldn't. For those of you who know anything about computer science, this is the 'bootstrap problem'. A computer (just the raw hardware) cannot run a program unless it is already running another program to allow it to interpret the first, and so on.

Perception cannot therefore be a passive matter of the accumulation of sensory information, but is an active process that constructs an understanding of the world from the available sensory input and a system of pre-existing assumptions about its nature. These assumptions may either be present from birth as part of our human nature, or may be developed as a result of earlier experience. However if empiricism presents us with the problem of understanding how we would ever come to know anything, this nativist view of the constructive nature of perception makes it sound as if we might just be making things up as we go along. Why is it that different people do not experience the world in quite different ways? Again, we will summarise several thousand years of philosophical tradition to say that this is indeed exactly what we do find. We can get some relief from this logical difficulty by remembering that our perceptual systems are a product of our evolutionary history and, generally speaking, evolution has favoured mechanisms which provide a relatively accurate picture of the outside world so that we will be able to behave in a sensible and adaptive way towards it. Our perceptions about the physical world appear to be in fairly close agreement with those of other people, but we may experience quite significant disagreement in our perceptions of the social world, and about the motives of those around us.

Notice too that evolution is not concerned with slavish physical accuracy in perception, but rather with providing an optimal level of accuracy to allow us to behave successfully in the world while working economically with the available mental processing power. Perceptual systems (indeed, all of our mental processing systems) take short cuts to reach their conclusions. These short cuts are sometimes referred to as heuristics, or 'rules of thumb'. Heuristics usually come to behaviourally accurate conclusions – evolutionary pressures ensure this – but sometimes result in rather peculiar conclusions, which we call illusions. We will return to illusions later, as sensory situations that produce illusory percepts can tell us a great deal about how the perceptual systems actually work in normal circumstances. Indeed, it is a frequent research approach in psychology to present the brain with circumstances that make it fail (too much to remember, for example, or information arriving at too great a rate), and to analyse the nature of the failure to further understand the normal functioning of the system under investigation.

We have already said that we perceive the world through the medium of our senses. We traditionally talk about the five senses, taking these to be touch, taste, smell, sight and hearing.

We will briefly explore the workings of the major organs of sensation.

VISION

The eye has often been compared to a camera, and the advent of digital photography makes this analogy even closer. Light from the world around us is focused through the lens system at the front of the eye and projected onto the retina at the rear of the eyeball. The retina is covered with sensitive cells of two different types, called rods and cones because of their shapes when viewed under a microscope. The relative density of cones is higher towards the centre of the retina. Rods are concerned with high-definition visual data collection and with colour vision. The density of rods is higher towards the edge of the retina and, because of the ways in which adjacent cells are connected together, this area of the retina is particularly sensitive in the detection of movement, or slight fluctuations in light level.

The fact that we have two eyes contributes a number of advantages. The slightly different views from the two eyes can, when correlated within the brain, provide information about three-dimensional space. This is known as binocular stereopsis. Close one eye, however, and you will not suddenly lose the impression of visual space in three dimensions. We will return to other sources of information about visual depth perception later. What you will notice if you only have information from one eye is a severe degradation in your night vision. Try working in illumination just bright enough for you to read comfortably, then shut, or cover, one eye. Reading will become noticeably more difficult, or even impossible. This is because the inputs from the two eyes contribute to a 'noise cancellation' system; if one eye 'drops a pixel' from one part of the visual scene, the chances are that the other eye can fill in the missing information.

Speaking of pixels, let us return to the analogy between the eye and a digital camera. Relatively inexpensive digital cameras have sensitive arrays of 4–5 megapixels, and arrays of 7–8 megapixels and above are commercially available at a price. With some crude approximations and simple arithmetic, one can come to the conclusion that the pixel density of the retina is close to that of a bottom-of-the-range digital camera. This would be to miss a few important points, however. First, the density of receptive cells on the retina is much higher at the centre (the fovea) than the periphery, so average pixel density tells us little about the workings of the eye. Second, that central region is constantly scanning over the field of view as it builds up a picture of the world. Unlike the camera, the receptor cells on the retina are connected to one another, and so what is happening to one cell influences how those round about it react. The interconnectivity in the periphery of the retina is particularly extensive, making this region very sensitive to low illumination and also very good at detecting movement. We can sum this up by saying that the digital camera merely records information, while the retina actively processes it.

HEARING

Our sense of hearing is dependent on our ability to detect minute vibrations transmitted through the air around us. These vibrations set up other, sympathetic vibrations in the eardrum that are transformed, via a system of bony levers, into a vibration along the length of a membrane curled up within the cochlea of the inner ear. Sensory cells cover this membrane and respond to distortion caused by the vibrations. How loud the sound is heard to be depends on the degree of distortion. The process by which the brain works out the pitch of the sound is a little harder to explain, but is still understandable in simple mechanical terms. Think about playing with a long rope, whipping one end up and down to send a wave along its length. If you have never done this, find a rope and try. If you move your arm rapidly up and down you will create a short wave (a high frequency) that will not get very far down the rope. A slow movement will produce a large wave (a low frequency) that will pass far further along. So it is for the membrane within the cochlea. Distortions at one end of the membrane specify high frequency sounds, while distortions along the length of the membrane specify low frequencies. This is a bit of an oversimplification, but it gives you the idea. It also gives you an insight into how a cochlear implant can assist with certain sorts of deafness. The implant bypasses the mechanical systems of the outer and middle ear, stimulating the cochlea directly.

Thinking about direct nerve stimulation like this brings us to an aside, and to an observation that has been described as the Law of Specific Nerve Energies. Put simply, what this means is that the sensory experience we have depends on which bit of the nervous system has been stimulated – and not on the nature of the energy that stimulated it. Stimulate the inner ear and we experience a sound, even if the source of the stimulation was electrical in nature. If we receive a blow to the back of the head (the location of the part of the brain that processes incoming visual information), we 'see stars'. Do not try this at home! There is a gentler experiment that you can try, however. Close your eyes in a relatively darkened environment and, very lightly and gently, apply pressure with your finger to your eyeball through your closed eyelid. You should 'see' a patch of light in your visual field. The light mechanical stimulus to the retina causes a visual percept without the involvement of any light. Where do you 'see' the light in relation to the point of pressure? Test your hypothesis by pressing (very gently, remember) at other points. What does this tell you about the eye? How does this link to what you know about how lenses work?

TOUCH AND PROPRIOCEPTION

From the description above you can see that our sense of hearing is just a highly evolved, sensitive and elaborated sense of touch. Our skin, particularly the skin of the hands, is richly supplied by sensory nerve endings and associated accessory structures which, when stimulated, give rise to the sensations of touch. Just what we experience is specified by the particular nerves that are stimulated. The simple experience of tactile contact is produced by structures which, when distorted by pressure to the surface of the skin, cause their associated nerve fibres to react. The particular feelings of heat or cold are produced by the response of more specialised accessory structures.

The term 'proprioception' refers to the business of keeping track of what is going on inside the body. For example, stretch receptors in joints and muscles can give the brain information about the movement of the limbs, and a specialised system within the inner ear conveys information about the orientation of the head with respect to gravity.

CHEMICAL SENSES

Our senses of taste and smell are closely linked, and are based on nervous responses to the presence of certain chemicals. The way in which the chemical senses work is closely analogous to the mechanisms by which nerves communicate with one another by the release and reception of chemical messengers. The molecular structure of the receptive site on the membrane of the sensory cell is of such a shape that certain molecules will 'fit' onto it, as a key fits into a lock. The right chemical (the key for that lock) will cause the receptor cell to respond.

The chemical senses carry information about 'value' in a very immediate way. Taste and smell tell us about things that we should be attracted to, and things that we should avoid. As was once memorably remarked, they convey information about 'gust and disgust'.

THE FIRST LABORATORY OF PSYCHOLOGY

Consideration of sensory experience in this way is a good opportunity to introduce a little bit of history. The first psychology laboratory was set up at the University of Leipzig in Germany in 1879 by Wilhelm Wundt. Wundt was the author of the very first textbook on psychology, *Principles of Physiological Psychology,* published in 1873. He was interested, among many more general things, in the way in which the elementary sensory events that he could describe from a physiological point of view gave rise to complex perceptions. The method for which he is particularly remembered is introspection (literally, 'looking inside'). Wundt trained observers to report and describe the sensory qualities of what they were experiencing while trying to ignore how these experiences made them think, or feel. This is not easy. Try it. Look at, listen to or touch the world around you. As I sit and write this, I hear the sound of the wind outside my office window and the siren of an emergency vehicle in the distance. I would be extremely hard pressed to describe these in terms of the component sounds that 'make up' this experience. Indeed, this was the experience of Wundt and his observers, and the methodology fell into disuse. Sensory experiences seem to be below the level of our conscious attention. We don't see patches of white, yellow and blue – we see a police car. Wundt's definition of psychology had been 'the science of immediate experience' but this came to be increasingly replaced by a psychology understood as 'the science of behaviour', giving less weight to people's descriptions of their experiences and more emphasis to what could be observed from the outside. Yet what Wundt and his followers did was to establish psychology as a scientific discipline, open to a scientific approach based on observable evidence rather than (or in addition to) the concern of philosophers, who approached it by reason and reflection.

SENSORY SYSTEMS

Considering the senses and sensory organs in isolation, then, is very much less than satisfactory. For example, to the traditional five senses we can also add the kinaesthetic sense, which refers to those mechanisms in our muscles and joints that contribute to the felt position of our bodies. Related to this is the information that is gathered from our inner ear about the force of gravity, which helps us to balance. The fine development of these senses of body position and orientation is vital in much skilled sporting performance.

Thinking about balance and body position, why is it that people often feel that they are about to lose their balance when they stand and look out from the top of a high building? This can be understood in terms of the contribution that the visual system makes to the control of balance through the detection of body sway. As we move through the world, changes in the relative positions of objects seen around us contribute to our sense of motion. This effect is termed motion parallax. The small movements of the head resulting from normal body sway result in small amounts of motion parallax information, thus helping us to correct the sway. It can be demonstrated that we sway more when we stand with our eyes shut than with our eyes open. And when we look out from a high vantage point there are frequently no nearby objects to provide us with this motion parallax information, thus contributing to the vertigo which some people experience so acutely. Motion sickness is also partially caused by a mismatch in information about body movement coming from our eyes and our ears. It is motion parallax, rather than binocular stereopsis which provides most information about three-dimensional space.

Another example of integration across the individual sensory systems would come from the remarkable phenomenon of facial vision sometimes reported by people who are totally blind. Blind individuals may describe being aware of objects in the environment in front of them that they can demonstrably not see, and are not close enough to touch. This ability can be understood to be a form of echo location system, analogous to that which is highly developed in bats and dolphins. Noises in the environment – caused, for example, by an ongoing conversation – bounce off the object and are detected as minute vibrations by the highly sensitive touch organs in the skin of the face.

Non-human animals can have sensory worlds that are quite different from our own. We have mentioned bats that can navigate in total darkness by the use of echo location. Some animals, like the electric eel, use the electric field that they create in the water around them as a means of remote detection of their prey. Honey bees have evolved a remarkable system of communicating the distance and direction of food sources from the colony home, a system dependent on the sensitivity of the bee's eye to polarised light patterns. Other animals have particularly acute chemical senses. Experiments have shown that dogs, for example, are able to discriminate between shapes in the dark on the basis of the smells wafting off them.

PARAPSYCHOLOGY

There has also been considerable research into phenomena collectively known as extrasensory perception (ESP). This term, refers to the gaining of understanding about the world through media beyond our natural senses. Examples of ESP include telepathy (the ability to communicate by thoughts alone), clairvoyance (the ability to see things in the future) and precognition (the ability to know about an event before it happens). The study of these and other paranormal experiences is called parapsychology or, perhaps more usefully, the psychology of anomalous experience. The study of such experiences does not imply that the researchers involved believe that the phenomena under consideration are a result of any supernatural or paranormal cause, although some parapsychologists are clearly approaching the topic as a search for the presence of some extrasensory medium. Others are seeking to understand, from the perspective of conventional psychology, 'how we know what isn't so'.

You will probably have perceived from the cautious tone of the previous few lines that the authors of this book take a rather sceptical position on paranormal phenomena. Our university, Edinburgh, has for some time been an important centre for the study of parapsychology, and there are many people working in the field – quite a number taking a sceptical stance – for whom we have the highest respect as scientists. Parapsychologists are often the most rigorous of psychologists in relation to their methodology and analysis of data, knowing that they have to be extremely thorough if they want to persuade the conventional scientific community. Our view would be that, while people clearly have anomalous experiences that they are inclined to interpret as having a basis beyond conventional human ability, these phenomena are indeed open to be understood in terms of complex, though natural, psychological processes.

For example, recent research has demonstrated that humans have exceptionally sophisticated abilities to perceive patterns of eye gaze in people they encounter. Specifically, we are extremely good at detecting when we are being looked at. Such an ability would be particularly useful from an evolutionary perspective in alerting us to a potential threat or a reproductive possibility, or simply in managing social interactions in a large group. This perceptual ability is rarely experienced on a conscious level, however, but rather as a vague awareness that we are being watched. Depending on the circumstances, this can give us a 'creepy feeling'.

There are many other situations in which one's experience of 'something odd' having happened can afford of a perfectly natural, though complex, explanation. One such example would be what has been termed 'the Bowery El Phenomenon'. Residents in the Bowery district of New York began to contact the police, reporting hearing noises in the night that had roused them from sleep. No evidence of intruders or other physical events could be found to explain the experiences. It was then noticed that the timing of the reports had a pattern, and was related to the schedule of the trains that used to run through the district on the recently dismantled elevated railway, known to locals as the 'El '. What the residents were perceiving was the *absence* of a regularly anticipated experience.

ILLUSION

Simpler examples of anomalous experience can be seen in what we frequently refer to as perceptual illusions. The most common illusions are those experienced in our optical system.

You may be familiar with many geometrical optical illusions from illustrations in books. (The internet is an excellent source of such illusions – simply search for 'optical illusions'. In particular, look for an illustration of the Hermann Grid.) Remember the example of the motion after-effect described in Chapter 4? The motion after-effect illusion and the Hermann Grid illusion both illustrate a very general aspect of the nervous system – that it responds to change, and pays less attention to a steady state. The system adapts to steady motion, and when that motion stops it registers a slight motion in the opposite direction due to momentary 'overcompensation'.

There are many after-effect illusions that you will be aware of. Stare fixedly at a red light for a few moments until it is switched off (you can do this trick with pedestrian crossing lights). You will be conscious of a green image where the red was. This is due to the fact that, in terms of the way in which the visual system codes colour, red is the 'opposite' of green.

AFFORDANCE

What the above examples suggest is that perception is not just a matter of passive reception of information but a complex construction of meaning based on evolutionary relevance, as well as our own past experience and memory. One of the most extreme statements of this view, and a very powerful and influential notion within the psychology of perception, is to be found in the idea of affordance developed by James Gibson. What Gibson proposed was that we directly perceive what he called 'affordances for action' in the outside world. We perceive through the medium of our senses – Gibson's work was primarily directed to the visual system – what it is that we can do. So if we look at the flat, textured surface at our feet we perceive that it affords support; it can be walked upon. A flat surface at about knee-height affords sitting. The handle of a door is of a size and position that it affords grasping, turning, pulling or pushing, and so on. The concept of affordances has been extended (some might say overextended) into many aspects of our interaction with the physical and social world, and the design of technology.

CONCLUSION

As we have seen, the study of perception is of fundamental importance in our understanding of how we come to know about truth and reality in the outside world. Yet the perceptual systems work by relative rather than absolute responding, and take many short cuts in the processing of incoming information. Perception is a constructive process, based on the available information but greatly influenced by past experience and expectations. For the most part these systems provide us with the accurate information upon which we base our actions. There is still sufficient uncertainty within the systems, however, to allow our higher thought processes and emotional states to greatly influence how we experience things.

FURTHER READING

Bruce, V. (1998), 'Fleeting images of shade: identifying people caught on video', *The Psychologist*, vol. 11, July, pp. 331–3
Since the early 1980s the study of the identification of people from their faces has become an important topic for those interested in perception and cognition. This article conveys succinctly why the human face is such an interesting object for psychologists to study. Interpersonal impression formation, the effects of attractiveness or disfigurement, the perception and expression of emotions, neonatal imitation and neuro-psychological impairments of social skills are amongst the many interesting and important topics looked at, where information from the face plays a vital role.

Morgan, M. (2003), *The Space Between Our Ears: How the Brain Represents Visual Space*, Oxford: Oxford University Press.

In this book Professor Michael Morgan explains how our brains interpret what we see. Using a wealth of sources from over the centuries, including philosophical writings, scientific thinking, experiments, passages from poems and novels and scenes from films, Morgan reveals the difficulties in working out exactly how we make and receive our visual perceptions.

Ramachandran, M. S. (2003), *The Emerging Mind* (BBC Reith Lectures), London: Profile Books Ltd.
(This series of lectures is also available to download and view video clips from www.bbc.co.uk/radio4/reith2003/) Professor Ramachandran is Director of the Centre for Brain and Cognition at the University of California at San Diego. His third lecture, on the nature of art, is particularly recommended.

Ward, J. (2003), 'State of the art – Synaesthesia', *The Psychologist*, vol. 16, April, pp. 196–9.
What colour is the letter A? What does the number 1 taste of? Does listening to music, eating food or speaking produce colours, shapes or textures? For most people, questions such as these will either yield a look of bewilderment or an emphatic 'No!' However, when the author posed this question to psychology undergraduates at University College London, as many as one per cent were certain that they experienced some of the effects suggested. These students may well have synaesthesia, the summoning up of other sensory modalities in addition to the primary sensation. This article is a good starting point on the topic.

6 COGNITIVE PSYCHOLOGY

In any scientific discipline there are fashionable and unfashionable areas and very often a particular branch of the subject assumes especial importance. In recent years such status has been attributed to cognitive psychology, and you will almost certainly carry out experiments in your practical course which engage with topics such as attention, memory, problem solving, thinking and language. It is also the area of psychology which is most closely associated with other disciplines such as artificial intelligence, informatics, linguistics and computer science. The common connection is understanding the theoretical basis of cognition, and building models of how the brain might undertake a task.

STUDIES OF ATTENTION

The breakthroughs which started the cognitive revolution in psychology originated in the problems faced by defence personnel in World War II. One particularly pressing issue was the need to understand more of the processes involved in staring at radar screens and correctly detecting an unpredictable signal which might be the blip of an approaching enemy aircraft. These studies, pioneered by a communications engineer, Colin Cherry, and an ex-RAF pilot and psychologist, Donald Broadbent, started the experimental study of attention. They involved listening to words played into one ear which the participants were asked to repeat aloud (speech shadowing), while in the other ear an unrelated series of words was played. This ingenious task, known as dichotic listening, enabled Cherry and Broadbent to assess how far participants were attending to the message, by measuring if they made any errors in their shadowing. The interesting finding was that if the participants were asked to report on what was happening in the unattended ear, they had virtually no knowledge. They did not detect switches from a male to a female voice, to another language or even to a meaningless sound such as reversed speech. If, however, the participant's own name was inserted into the unattended ear, it might cause an inadvertent switch to shadowing messages in this same ear.

These experiments are described in Broadbent's classic book *Perception and Communication*, which although published in 1958 is still well worth consulting. In this work Broadbent also developed his selective filter theory of attention, to account for how the brain deals with the information overload from several conflicting messages arriving simultaneously at different sense organs. Each sense is spoken of in engineering terms as a channel, and his innovation was to suggest a single central information channel of limited capacity within the brain. The filter permits only one channel to be attended to at a time, with information in the unattended channel held briefly in a short-term memory store. Although we are conscious of only the information in one channel, this is not to say that the unattended channel can be without influence on behaviour, as in the contentious area of subliminal perception. Earlier, more outrageous claims that subliminal messages promoting commercial products – projected subliminally onto cinema screens – increased the sale of popcorn and soft drinks, are certainly untrue. There is good experimental evidence, however, that simultaneous words in an unattended channel can be shown to influence what people report hearing in the attended channel.

STUDIES OF MEMORY

Memory has a long history of laboratory experimentation, starting with a famous series of experiments conducted by Hermann Ebbinghaus in 1885. Ebbinghaus attempted to look at the memory for artificially constructed lists of nonsense syllables (such as zak, guj, vek and lur), for which there were no previous associations. He then plotted his own recall of these lists over many days, resulting in so-called curves of forgetting. Although flawed, the experiments are important for their first usage of nonsense syllables, still widely employed today in memory experiments, and for demonstrating that quantitative methods could be applied to understanding higher mental processes.

Two basic experiments demonstrate some important characteristics of human memory. The first involves participants reading aloud a series of three-letter nonsense trigrams, such as GUJ. Immediately after saying each one, they are presented with a three-digit number, say 593, and asked to count backwards in threes. They are stopped after various intervals of time, ranging from 5 to 60 seconds, and asked to recall the trigram. The purpose of the counting backwards procedure is to stop participants rehearsing the trigram mentally to themselves. The memory for such trigrams is found to decay very rapidly over about 40 seconds until it reaches a plateau. This classic experiment reveals that memory for items which cannot be rehearsed is rather brief, and known as short-term memory (STM). It is why if you are trying to remember a telephone number you have just looked up, and someone asks you a question, often you will no longer correctly recall it. The time spent dealing with the question asked of you is sufficient for the short-term memory trace of the digits in the telephone number to decay to nothing.

The second experiment involves asking people to read or listen to a list of twenty common words, and at the end of the list to try to recall as many of them as possible by writing them all down. If we do this with perhaps twenty people, and plot their results as a percentage of correctly recalled words as a function of their position on the list, then we will find that memory for items, at the beginning of the list, typically the first two items, is significantly better than the later words. However, the last four or five words are recalled better than the preceding words in the middle of the list. If we had asked our participants to start counting backwards at the end of the word list as in the first experiment, then we would find that their memory for the last few words is no better than the middle of the list. Such a result, known as the Serial Position Effect, illustrates two basic kinds of memory: items which are held briefly in a time-limited short-term store, the STM, and a more permanent representation known as long-term memory (LTM). The better recall of the first two items in the list is known as the primacy effect, while the better recall of the last few items is known as the recency effect.

These experiments led to the formulation of the first box models of memory in which information was believed to pass initially through a short-term store and would only enter into a permanent LTM if actively rehearsed, or if particular importance was attached to it. An example of the latter might be a 'flash-bulb memory', so called because it refers to our retaining a clear impression of the circumstances when we first heard of, or experienced, an event of deep personal or emotional importance. This was first noted when people were asked to describe what they were doing when they first heard of the assassination of US president John F. Kennnedy in 1964. You may have a flash-bulb memory of where you were when you heard of the death of Princess Diana, in 1997.

Laboratory and Field Studies

In memory research there are two very distinct lines of investigation, one laboratory based, using computers for high-level control of stimulus materials, the other looking at more naturalistic memory such as the flash-bulb effect. This second approach can be traced back to Sir Frederick Bartlett's work on recalling stories, something all of us would feel to be a familiar problem. Bartlett emphasised what he called 'effort after meaning', which we can understand as putting things into a context. A well-known experiment here involves participants reading a short account which is either entitled 'Washing Clothes' or 'Burgling a House'. They are then asked a series of questions in the recall stage of the experiment – half the questions based on a burglar's perspective of the story and half based on the laundry perspective. Memory was much better for the questions appropriate to the title, even though the stories were identical. This underlines the importance of the initial encoding of information, and the selective processing which may be involved. It leads us onto a consideration of how memory can be distorted, and how the way we are questioned about events influences our recall, which has been elegantly demonstrated by Elisabeth Loftus in a series of experiments examining the problems of eyewitness testimony.

If volunteers view a film of a car accident and are then subsequently asked to estimate the speed at which the car was travelling, the level of speed they guess at increases according to whether the question asks if the car 'hits', 'collides' or 'smashes' into another car. Subsequent memories of the film are changed by this different verb usage, even though the film does not show broken glass. Viewers are far more likely to say they saw broken glass if initially they estimated speed on the basis of smashing into rather than being hit by the other car. The real life analogy to this is the court room situation where a judge must eliminate the use of 'leading questions' which make assumptions ahead of direct evidence.

Improving memory

There are many examples of people showing exceptional memory. It is not unusual, for instance, for devout Muslims to be able to recite the Koran, and in India the entire text of the epic story the *Mahabharata*. Professional memory experts, or mnemonists, who perform seemingly impossible feats such as memorising strings of thousands of digits or hundreds of related words make use of a few simple techniques. Using functional brain imagery, Eleanor Maguire and colleagues from University College London studied eight leading contestants in the annual World Memory Championships. They found that, while memorising, the participants showed activity in three brain regions that become active during movements and navigation tasks but are not normally active during simple memory tests. Seven of the eight contestants used a strategy in which they placed items to be remembered along a visualised route. To remember the sequence of an entire pack of playing cards, for example, they assigned to each card an identity, for instance an object or person, and as they flicked through the cards they made up a story based on a sequence of interactions between these characters and objects at sites along a well-known route. Actors use a related technique: they attach emotional meaning to what they say, on the basis that we remember highly emotional moments better than less emotionally loaded ones. Professional actors also seem able to link words with movements, remembering lines accompanied by action significantly better than those delivered while static, even months after a show has closed. Non-actors can benefit by adopting a similar technique. Students who paired their words with previously learned actions could reproduce 38 per cent of them after only five minutes, whereas rote learners only managed 14 per cent.

Insights from Brain Damage

Neuropsychological case descriptions have been of particular importance in supporting or rebutting hypotheses about cognitive processes of language processing and memory, formulated from laboratory experiments with healthy volunteers. There are a number of recognised memory systems replacing the classic STM/LTM distinction of forty years ago. Short-term memory is now thought of as a working memory involved in any mental activity extended in time, such as the production and comprehension of language. These processes are rarely compromised as a result of ageing or of brain damage, and STM is a very robust system by comparison with LTM. There are now recognised to be many divisions of the latter, starting with the intriguing discovery that cases such as H. M. (see Chapter 4), those suffering from dense global amnesia and unable to form any new long-term memories, are able to learn and retain their improved performance on certain kinds of tasks. These protected tasks involve the performance of skilled movements such as the ability to learn to do mirror drawing. Here the task is to draw in between the double outlines of a geometric pattern such as a star, not touching either of the contours and viewing one's hand indirectly in a mirror, with a screen preventing direct observance of hand movements. The trick is to learn to move one's hands in the opposite direction to that intended, as one sees the mirror reversal of one's actual hand movements. H. M. was able to acquire this skill over two or three days and perform at a level similar to controls, but on each occasion he professed ignorance of what he had to do, and denied having seen the test apparatus on previous occasions. He exhibited a dissociation between his conscious awareness (previous familiarity with the task) and his performance, which improved and was maintained across practice sessions. This preserved memory has been called procedural to distinguish it from declarative memory, which is that which we can consciously recall and comment on. In the case of H. M., his declarative memory was of life events before his surgery; whereas his procedural memory allowed him to perform the actions, rather than giving him the ability to describe them.

UNDERSTANDING LANGUAGE PROCESSES

How we produce and understand language, and the relationship between language and thinking, are two important branches of cognitive psychology. When behaviourism was the dominant paradigm in psychology there was virtually no interest in language by psychologists, and it was not until the middle of the twentieth century that linguistic research took off. The impetus was the controversy concerning the relationship between language and thought, and the impact of the ideas of Benjamin Lee Whorf and his hypothesis of linguistic relativity. In its extreme form this stated that language determined thinking, a view now largely rejected. Thinking is apparent at an earlier developmental stage than language in the human child. Jean Piaget argued that language in young children builds on cognitive abilities developed during the pre-language sensorimotor period (see Chapter 7). Language is therefore the servant of thought rather than its master. Children who participate in a conservation task can be classified as conservers or non-conservers. Conservation tasks are those which test a child's understanding that certain properties of objects (such as volume, mass of number) remain unchanged when the objects' appearances are changed in some superficial way. Conservers correctly assert that when a quantity of water is poured from a short fat container into a long thin one, it remains the same. Children who say this are more linguisticly competent than the non-conservers, who make comments such as 'it's [the vessel] tall and thin, this is short but it's wide'. In experiments, teaching the non-conservers an appropriate conservation-relevant language only produced improvements on the task in some 10 per cent of subjects, showing that, here, the acquisition of appropriate linguistic skills did not facilitate thought. The link between linguistic competence and conservation is due to the fact that mastery of the cognitive skills involved in conservation facilitates learning the relative linguistic terms, and not vice versa.

Although we can reject the notion that language determines thinking, there is no doubt that it can influence how we think about the world (Geary, 1995). Children from Asian countries such as China perform better on tests of mathematical skills like counting, subtraction and addition than English-speaking children. A likely explanation for this difference involves the words and symbols the languages use to represent numbers. In Chinese it is much easier to learn the base-10 number system, especially from 10 to 100. English speakers, on the other hand, have to learn words such as sixteen, eleven and twelve, which have no conceptual relation to the base-10 model; in Chinese the equivalents are 'ten six, ten one and ten two'.

The complexity of participating in an ordinary conversation is apparent once we recognise its cognitive, linguistic and communicative components. Most of the time we effortlessly retrieve words from memory and produce them in a correct sequence, articulating the sounds such that listeners recognise what we are saying. Language has a syntax: the sounds and words are strung together by speakers and parsed by listeners in accordance with the vocabulary and grammar of the language being spoken. Finally, to get across our meaning, we adjust what we say according to what we know of our listeners. The errors made in this process are instructive and tell psycholinguists a good deal about the process of speech production – sometimes we are literally lost for words and suffer agonies as we attempt to locate the correct term, which we say is 'on the tip of my tongue'. Here is how one of psychology's founding fathers, William James, described the experience:

> Suppose we try to recall a forgotten name. The state of our consciousness is peculiar. There is a gap therein: but no mere gap. It is a gap that is intensely active. A sort of wraith of the name is in it, beckoning us in a given direction, making us at moments tingle with the sense of our closeness, and then letting us sink back without the longed-for term. If wrong names are proposed to us, this singularly definite gap acts immediately so as to negate them. They do not fit into its mould. And the gap of one word does not feel like the gap of another, all empty of content as both might seem necessarily to be when described as gaps. (James 1890, vol. I, pp. 251–2)

Surprisingly, even if unable to report anything about what the word sounds like when in this state, speakers are able to report on specific grammatical properties of the word that cannot be derived from its meaning. Our knowledge of words seems to come in pieces, and neurophysiological indicators of semantic retrieval processes are fractions of a second in front of phonological retrieval processes. The effortlessness of speech production turns out to be a complicated assembly of semantic, syntactic and phonological properties of words, produced not simultaneously but in quick succession.

FURTHER READING

Berry, Dianne (2002), 'Donald Broadbent', *The Psychologist*, vol. 15, August, pp. 402–5.

A good account of the importance of Broadbent to British psychology, this article is a clear demonstration of Broadbent's maxim that 'a good psychology is an applied psychology'.

Geary, D. (1995), 'Reflections of evolution and culture in children's cognition: implications for mathematical instruction and development', *American Psychologist*, vol. 50, pp. 24–37.

James, W. (1890), *The Principles of Psychology*, New York: Doves publications.

We include this reference as one of the all-time classics in psychology, which marked a real turning-point in the development of the subject. At some stage in your undergraduate career you should definitely browse the contents of this book.

Pinker, S. (1994), *The Language Instinct*, New York: William Morrow.

This is simply the best popular work on linguistics around, and if you are only going to read one book on the subject then Pinker's should be the one. He covers difficult topics such as arguments for the innateness of language, why humans have a common 'universal grammar', the relationship between language and thought, language acquisition by infants and the evolution of language. Pinker writes with humour and peppers his work with topical issues and literary asides.

Robertson, H. Ian (2003), 'The absent mind, attention and error', *The Psychologist*, vol. 16, September, pp. 476–9.

The author considers some of the neuropsychological research into people who have attentional problems following strokes or accidents.

Wetherick, Norman (2003), 'Against cognitive psychology', *The Psychologist*, vol. 16, January, pp. 22–3.

This article in the 'Personal Space' column of the journal allows members to express their own individual prejudices and is included here to show that controversy is always not far from the surface in psychology.

7 DEVELOPMENTAL PSYCHOLOGY

Developmental psychology is mainly concerned with the early years of life rather than adulthood. Although 'Lifespan development' is taught on some degree courses, in most the emphasis will be very much on the first ten years of life. The reasons for this are not hard to find. Some of the most interesting questions concern the extent to which our characteristics and behaviour are inborn or result from experience – the nature/nurture debate (see page 47). This exercised the mind of King James IV of Scotland (ruled 1488–1553) to the extent that he caused two children to be brought up by a deaf and dumb guardian and, to ensure their isolation from a speaking population, housed them on the uninhabited island of Inchkeith in the Firth of Forth. The outcome of this sad experiment is not known – one account told how the children were heard to speak in Hebrew, which perhaps illustrates the caution with which we should treat such tales. There are several other well-documented accounts of such 'feral' children, brought up in either severely deprived or unusual circumstances. The best known is probably that of Victor, the wild boy of Aveyron in southern France on which the film director Francois Truffaut based his film *L'Enfant Sauvage*.

The Swiss philosopher Jean-Jacques Rousseau (1712–78) believed that upbringing and learning experiences had almost no role in shaping development in the early years, and in his most famous work, *Emile*, put forward the view of children as innately good with little need for moral guidance. In sharp contrast, the British empiricist John Locke (1632–1704) described the child as a blank slate onto which could be etched characteristics resulting from the child's unique experiences. His view allowed no room for the idea that innate factors have any important role to play in psychological development.

In 1890, William James echoed such views when he famously remarked that, for a newborn baby, the world is a 'buzzing, blooming confusion, where the infant is seized by eyes, ears, nose and entrails all at once.' In fact, we now hold almost the opposite view to that of James, that far from being essentially passive with little awareness of self or external reality, the infant has a high degree of competence in both perception and cognition. As one influential exponent of this view put it, 'the newborn infant starts life as an extremely competent social organism, an extremely competent learning organism, an extremely competent perceiving organism' (Bower, 1979).

THE WORK OF PIAGET

The Swiss biologist Jean Piaget (1896–1980) was the first to describe the stages of infant development and identify distinct modes of operation. Many of his findings developed from observations of his own children, and his descriptions remain the basis for modern research on mental development in infancy. Piaget believed that infants construct their knowledge about the world through their own actions, and that up to about eight months of age thought *is* action. From birth the infant possesses a number of innate reflexes, which become generalised away from the original initiating stimuli. For example, babies have a sucking reflex which was evolved for feeding but quickly applies to other objects such as the baby's hand and fingers. As the baby sucks her hand she finds out information about it. Piaget called this the assimilation of information about the hand.

Piaget's most famous demonstrations, showing that infants acquire the ability to think by interacting with the world in increasingly more complex ways over the first year of life, were published in 1937 as *The Child's Construction of Reality*. In this book he considers how babies think about inanimate objects such as toys, apples and bottles. Whereas adults know that these objects are permanent and do not change their shape, for the baby this is not the case. A rattle does not have a permanent existence but is part of the structure of the baby's own acts. So what the baby does to a toy rattle is what the baby thinks about the rattle – objects are said to possess a motor meaning and, because of this, have no permanence. What Piaget meant by this was that when the baby shakes the rattle it represents her thinking about the rattle. If the rattle is hidden then for the baby it effectively ceases to exist. Recognising that this is not the case only develops towards the end of the second year of life, and is a significant liberation from the physical world. According to Piaget the object is now freed from both action and perception. The baby conceives of the object as permanent and can now form symbols or internal representations of it.

Even though Piaget is one of psychology's intellectual giants he has not gone unchallenged. A particularly interesting theoretical alternative is that developed by Tom Bower and colleagues at Edinburgh University. Bower reasoned that the baby does know where the object is but does not know how to get to it. This is very different to Piaget's argument that the baby does not attempt to find objects hidden under a cloth because, for that baby, they literally no longer exist. To distinguish between these two explanations we need a behaviour other than hand searching (which the baby cannot do) to show the baby knows the object still exists. Bower suggested this could be done by looking at the eye movements of the baby and by any expressions of surprise.

He showed the baby a toy and then hid it from view by placing a screen between the toy and the baby. Next, he compared the baby's reaction when the screen was removed depending upon whether the object was still there or had vanished. If babies imagine that covered things disappear, as Piaget suggested, then the reappearance of a hidden object should surprise them more than evidence that it really has vanished. Alternatively, if they really believe the toy is still there behind the screen, they will be more surprised when the screen is raised and the toy has vanished! Using a change of heart rate as a measure of surprise, Bower found that babies were less surprised to see the hidden toy again than to find it had gone. Furthermore, if babies saw a toy moving at a constant speed and then disappearing behind a screen, they continued to track the object with their eyes (eye movements recorded with sophisticated eye tracking instruments have an important role in many other areas of psychology, particularly in understanding how we process and understand written words) and registered surprise if the toy did not reappear at the correct moment at the other side of the screen. Both these ingenious experiments suggest that babies know that an object still exists even when it is out of sight.

THE BABY AS A COMMUNICATOR

In the early 1970s a view of the infant began to emerge which suggested that babies were well able to distinguish between people and objects. Much of this work came from the frame-by-frame analysis of videotapes depicting mothers speaking to and playing with their babies. Focusing on the movements of the baby – its hands, feet, arms, legs and general body movements – while the baby listened to its mother's speech and looked at her face, researchers such as Colwyn Trevarthen at Edinburgh University observed a synchronisation between mother and baby – a taking of turns, almost like a dance. Two-month-old babies appear to engage with their mothers in regular conversation-like exchanges, during which Trevarthen believes that the infant is the prime controller of events. Indeed, he has stated that babies are born 'with mysterious but very powerful psychological mechanisms that ensure interpersonal and social co-operation in human intelligence. [This] gives humans adaptive domination over all other forms of life, and unlimited power to acquire and transmit techniques for mastery of the environment' (quoted in T.G. Bever 1982, Regressions in Mental Development: Basic Phenomena and Theories. Erlbaum, Hillsdale NJ).

Humans are the most expressive of all species. It was Charles Darwin who first described the universality of the six primary facial expressions of joy, disgust, anger, fear, surprise and sadness across many different cultures around the world. Babies appear to imitate facial actions posed by models, such as sticking out their tongues and pursing their lips. Mothers often remark that their newborn baby looks sad, happy or is smiling – this may be put down to harmless self-deception, but experiments (see Field et al., 1982) with infants as young as 36 hours show that they are indeed able to imitate facial expressions. A series of three expressions – happy, sad and surprised – were posed by an adult and observed by 74 neonates, with both the baby's and the model's faces video-taped simultaneously using a split-screen technique. Judges then coded the facial expressions of the infants and looked for matches to the model. The chance probability of guessing the facial expression correctly would be 33 per cent. In fact, 'sur-prised' was correctly guessed on 76 per cent of trials, 'happy' on 58 per cent, and 'sad' on 59 per cent. Videotapes of the model's face eliminated shaping or reinforcing the neonates' responses as a possible explanation for this result.

But if babies can imitate an adult's action, does this mean that they understand it? The authors reached the more modest conclusion that there is an innate ability to compare the visual information from facial expressions with the muscular move-ments involved in matching that expression. A split-screen video technique, whereby the face of the mother and the infant are seen side by side at exactly the same point in time, allows experimenters to investigate how babies react to interruptions in dialogues with their mothers. If the mother suddenly ceases to talk with her baby or looks distressed, then two-month-old infants will turn away and become upset. Trevarthen believes this is very strong evidence that babies can perceive the underlying mental state and feelings behind their mothers' expressions.

BONDING AND ATTACHMENT

The early 1970s also saw the development of a very influen-tial view that, for new mothers to fall in love with their babies (referred to as maternal bonding), it was essential that only minimal separation from their babies should occur soon after birth. Technically, maternal bonding has come to mean a rapid and irreversible change said to take place in the mother within a period immediately following birth and which lasts no more than a few hours or days at the most. During this time prolonged contact between mother and baby must occur if maternal feelings are to be properly mobilised. This 'super-glue' theory of maternal love, first put forward by two pediatricians, Marshall Klaus and John Kennell proved very influential, and failure to bond properly was frequently cited as the reason for all kinds of problems ranging from failure to thrive in infancy to cases of child abuse and adolescent delinquency. In one New York hospital this belief reached such heights of absurdity that mothers who had not held their babies after birth were given Polaroid photographs to look at so they could bond adequately!

The origins of bonding theory lie in work with animals, where there is good evidence for such a critical period in the formation of maternal attachment to the newborn. Many careful studies in the past two decades, however, have shown that there is no evidence of any long-term effects of enforced separation in the period immediately after birth. Hence a generation of doctors and nurses can be relieved of guilty feelings with the necessary forced separation following caesarian section deliveries or illness at birth. It is interesting that the ideas centred around maternal bonding, although without scientific foundation, revolutionised practice in postnatal wards, causing babies to sleep in cots at the side of their mothers. (For a good account of this controversy, see Schaffer, 1990.)

THEORY OF MIND

How infants understand their social world, in particular their relationship to other people, and whether they have an awareness of the mental state of others, are currently hot research topics. A first stage in this process is the development of self-recognition, illustrated in what has become known as the 'red nose' experiment. Infants aged between nine and twenty-four months were able to look at themselves in a mirror after they had had a small amount of rouge applied to the tip of their noses. Only the older infants touched their own noses when they looked in the mirror – the implication being that they had had an awareness of self in terms of understanding that this was their own reflection, and that the presence of the red spot was something different and unexpected.

Premack and Woodruff (1978) attempted to test whether chimpanzees have a theory of mind, their paper being published in a journal which also included the responses of other scientists. It was suggested in this peer commentary that chimpanzees and children could be tested to see if they had a theory of mind by giving them a false belief task. The essence of such a task is that the observer is privy to some crucial information that the subject does not have. If the observer has a theory of mind then they will be able to see that the behaviour of the subject will be consistent with their lack of information rather than with the information known to the observer. One such task, known as the Sally-Anne test, has been developed for use with preschool children. The child is shown a scene where a doll called Sally hides a marble and then leaves the room. A second doll, called Anne, moves the marble to a different hiding place while Sally is out of the room. The child is then asked to say where Sally will look for the marble when she comes back into the room. Three-year-olds almost always fail such tasks, predicting that Sally will look for the marble in the new location rather than in the original one in which she placed it and where she would expect it to be. Four- and five-year-olds will, however, pass the test as they are able to distinguish between their own knowledge and that of another person.

Autistic children seem to have a special difficulty with such 'Theory of Mind' tasks. High functioning autistic children with a normal intelligence range can be tested with the Sally-Anne task and invariably fail it. This has led some researchers to believe that autistic children have a specific deficit for which the general Theory of Mind does not allow.

THE LIMITS OF UNDERSTANDING

You may well be asking at this point whether some of the problems outlined above are more a consequence of the young child's limited language development – and hence misunderstanding of what is asked – rather than any lack of competence. This is clearly of especial importance in developmental psychology. Depending on how the task is presented or how the question is asked, children will either fail in Piagetian-type conservation tasks or demonstrate understanding. For example, a typical conservation of quantity task might ask the child whether there is more or less water in the new container when water is poured from a short fat vessel into a tall thin one. But if the experimenter provides a reason for pouring the water from one to the other – for instance, there is a crack in the original container or it is dirty – then the children answer correctly in the latter case and incorrectly in the standard test. They have reached understanding because the task makes human sense to them.

This is particularly clear in a final study from Edinburgh on number conservation (McGarrigle and Donaldson, 1974, described in Donaldson, 1978) – the 'naughty teddy' experiment. As in the original Piaget study, the experimenters arranged an equal number of counters in two parallel rows. The children were encouraged to move the counters until they agreed there was the same number in each row. Then a glove puppet, naughty teddy, manipulated by one of the experimenters appeared and was made to move the counters until one row was longer than the other, although the number of counters remained the same in each. The children were then asked if the two rows had the same or a different number of counters. In the original Piagetian version, children aged between four and six years of age thought that the number had changed and there were more counters in the longer row. But when naughty teddy was responsible for the change, they correctly answered that the number was the same.

Awareness of the limits of children's understanding is an essential part of a teacher's training, and everyone involved in the care and instruction of nursery and primary school children will benefit from acquiring some basic understanding of developmental psychology. Many of the better self-help books about childcare and development have good accounts of children's learning abilities. Doctors, nurses and other health professionals, together with those who need to question children as witnesses in criminal justice courts, all belong to professions where understanding child psychology is of great importance.

FURTHER READING

Bennett, Mark (2004), 'Children and social identity', *The Psychologist*, vol. 17, September, pp. 512–14.
This article examines research in the neglected area of the social self – in other words, the groups children identify with. It is based on asking children open-ended questions about identity.

Bower, T. G. R. (1979), *A Primer of Infant Development*, San Francisco: Freeman.

Coyne, M. Sarah (2004), 'Indirect aggression on screen: a hidden problem?', *The Psychologist*, vol. 17, December, pp. 688–90.
Psychologists have studied the effects of watching violence on television and cinema screens for the last fifty years. Early studies were criticised for failing to establish that television has a direct effect on aggressive behaviour, but research within the past two decades has demonstrated such an effect. Most findings indicate that watching violence influences children to become more aggressive, either in their attitudes or their actual behaviour.

Donaldson, M. (1978), *Children's Minds*, London: Fontana.
This is a modern classic in developmental psychology. The author disagreed with Jean Piaget's methods of investigating egocentricity, having herself come to different results when applying a social dimension to the tasks she gave to preschoolers. As Donaldson put it, the preschoolers' inability to perform Piaget's tasks was due to their difficulties with understanding or abstracting the actual questions, and not to their egocentricity or lack of logical skills.

Dunn, Judy (2004), *Children's Friendships: The Beginnings of Intimacy*. Oxford: Blackwell.
Professor Judy Dunn, of King's College London's Social, Genetic and Developmental Psychiatry Research Centre, is a leading international authority on child development. In this book she stresses the importance of friendships to young children and considers the implications of friendship for our understanding of children's development more generally. As well as discussing the practical implications for parents, teachers and other people who care for children, she considers how to help children with friendship difficulties and what to do about 'trouble-making' friendships and bullying.

Field, T. M., Woodson, R., Greenberg, R., Cohen, D. (1982), 'Discrimination and imitation of facial expression by neonates', *Science*, vol. 218, pp. 179–81.
Goswami, Usha (2003), 'How to beat dyslexia', *The Psychologist*, vol. 16, September, pp. 462–5.
This article considers how the rhyme and rhythm of different languages may be the key to understanding dyslexia. Children who grow up speaking English have greater difficulty in achieving particular standards of reading ability than children learning to read German, Finnish, Italian, Spanish or Greek. Goswami examines how nursery songs and clapping games may have an important developmental impact on literacy.

James, Oliver (2003), *They F*** You Up: How to Survive Family Life*, London: Bloomsbury.
Oliver James is a child psychologist turned writer, journalist and TV documentary producer and presenter. His book is a lively – if personal – view of the family influences which mould children, and has lively biographical sketches of contemporary figures in politics and the media.

Premack, D. and Woodruff, G. (1978), 'Does the chimpanzee have a theory of mind?', *Behavioural and Brain Sciences* vol. 1, pp. 515–26.
Schaffer, H. R. (1990), *Making Decisions about Childern*, Oxford: Blackwell.

8 SOCIAL PSYCHOLOGY

Social psychology concerns itself with our interactions and relationships with other people. Some social psychological research examines how we as individuals feel and think about, and act towards, others that we encounter in the world. Other research takes the social group as the basic unit of analysis, investigating how the behaviour of groups can best be understood. Social psychology is perhaps the area of psychology that most typifies the lay person's view of the discipline.

SOCIAL PERCEPTION

An important area of social psychology deals with the way in which we perceive, and therefore react to, the people that we encounter. In the social world, as in all other areas of our psychological functioning, the brain is adept at taking in a large amount of information and coming rapidly to decisions. This means that we use 'rules of thumb' in our reasoning (as we discussed in Chapter 5) rather than strict logic. It also means that our decisions are based on a series of assumptions that may be more or less valid in any given circumstance, laying us open to the danger of prejudice. Indeed, one can argue that all social perception involves prejudice, in that we make decisions about how people are likely to behave towards us based on very partial information. The strength of this system is that it enables us to act quickly in a world full of complex information; the danger is that we may jump to inappropriate conclusions. Today's urban dwellers live in a world full of significant risks due to the behaviour of other people. It is important to be able to detect these risks quickly to be able to avoid or minimise them. At the same time, our world is threatened by social and racial fear and intolerance that can be fuelled by our more elementary human nature. It is to be hoped that an understanding of the processes of social perception will help us to become more aware of some of our less well-grounded assumptions, and to reflect on and question them.

PROCESSES OF ATTRIBUTION

One of the rules of thumb that we use to simplify judgements in social settings is to ascribe basic motivations to people based on the behaviours that we see. This is a process that is referred to as attribution. For example, from a whole constellation of information, such as body posture, eye gaze, facial expression, tone of voice and the meaning of what is being said, we may judge someone to be friendly towards us. We therefore do not need to store and process the details of their behaviour, but rather simply work with the powerful simplifying assumption 'friend'. From a similar array of information we may conclude that someone is not warmly disposed to us, and sum this up as 'non-friend' or 'threat'. Subsequent information is then understood in that context, so that we react quite differently to the same behaviour from two different people. Think of how you would feel about a joke at your expense made by a friend, as opposed to someone that you do not regard as such.

There are biases built into the attributions that we make about people. The good news is that our initial biases when encountering new people are positive. Put crudely, we expect others to be like us, and to share our views and beliefs. First impressions are indeed, therefore, very important. After initial encounters with people we tend to give greater weight to evidence of negative attributes. We also tend to reason by paying more attention to evidence that supports our judgements than to evidence that would tend to disconfirm them. This means that it is easier for random events to sour a positive relationship than for a poor relationship to be improved by positive evidence against an earlier judgement.

Our social judgements are also aided and simplified by the use of organising frameworks known as schemas. One such schema would be the notion of 'balance'. Put simply, we expect to like the people who are liked by others whom we like. Or, alternatively, we expect to dislike the people who are liked by others whom we dislike. You can see at once that these relationships do not necessarily follow, but also that they are likely to be good predictors. Such schemas are simplifying assumptions that help to reduce the cognitive load imposed by the processing of complex social information. Prejudices of this sort may stick very quickly to organising categories that are defined by physical characteristics such as language, skin colour or facial features, conveying information about ethnicity.

The attributions that we make about people's motives can be located either internally or externally to the individual, and there will be a bias in how these are made. When someone we already feel warmly disposed to behaves badly towards us, we are likely to attribute their behaviour to the circumstances in which they find themselves: perhaps they have had a bad day at work or they have family worries. On the contrary, negative behaviour in someone we are not well disposed to is more likely to be attributed internally; that is, is due to undesirable qualities intrinsic to the person. Social perceptions may be highly differentiated at times, and the more we get to know someone, the more subtle will become our analysis and understanding of their strengths and weaknesses. We may believe, for example, that a particular friend is generally loyal and to be trusted, but that he is also a terrible gossip and therefore perhaps not one to whom we would first give personal news of a sensitive nature.

Social perceptions will be further influenced by our membership of, or exclusion from, social groups. For example, there is reason to give some 'slack' to a member of our own social group who appears to be behaving badly towards us. There is a motive to set aside, or at least moderate to some extent, our own judgements in order to preserve the cohesion of the group. On the other hand, there is no reason to be

generous to members of another group, and thereby potentially put ourselves at risk.

It is important to remember that the above generalisations
are based on statistical analyses from a wide variety or experimental, or quasi-experimental, research studies. All else being
equal, these patterns of bias will exist, but this is not to say that
all people will inevitably react in these ways. Understanding
these naturally occurring patterns of likelihood may help us to
some extent to free ourselves from the prejudices that we might
otherwise give in to.

THE IMPACT OF INFORMATION TECHNOLOGY

Whole new areas of concern for psychologists have been
opened up by computers and associated forms of information
and communications technologies (ICT). Cognitive psychology has traditionally made contributions to the design of
technologies, working with engineers to improve their usability and usefulness. The field of human-computer interaction
(HCI) has developed out of collaborations between psychology and computer science, and is concerned with the design
of interfaces which make complex technologies easy to use.

Social psychology has come more recently to the study of
ICT and its uses. We will mention two topics of research here.
One quite obvious new area of interest for social psychology has come with the rapid growth of technological systems
as mediators of communication. The other, perhaps more
surprising, findings have come from research which can be
summed up in the phrase 'computers as social actors'.

Communication Through Technologies

The growth of the internet, and its use as a medium of
social communication, has been staggering over recent years.
Computer-mediated communications (CMC) took off in a big
way in the UK in the autumn of 1994. We date this quite

particularly because we were involved with an 'e-mail for all' initiative in our institution that just anticipated this national trend. Electronic mail (e-mail), and the opportunities made available by the World Wide Web, made computers relevant to many people for the first time. Add to these the technologies of instant messaging (systems like Microsoft Messenger), internet chat rooms and, of course, the possibility of text messages between mobile phones and we can see that technology plays an increasingly important part in many people's social lives.

We mentioned that our institution was among the earliest in the UK to provide unlimited electronic mail access for our students. Some institutions were rather more hesitant, and part of this reluctance was based on fears that the facilities might be misused. There were stories around that the anonymity of e-mail encouraged inappropriate extremes of communication, particularly the aggressive or abusive behaviour known as 'flaming'. While these extreme fears were completely unfounded (although there are always some idiots around!), it is true that CMC can be shown to reduce some of the social inhibitions that can occur in face-to-face encounters. CMC in commercial organisations has been said to 'flatten the hierarchies' which previously existed in conventional models of line management. Employees appeared more able to communicate with senior colleagues, expressing opinions and offering suggestions. It has been observed, too, that women were able to use e-mail to good effect to get around the intimidation that they often encountered in face-to-face interactions with their male colleagues.

One influential analysis of both the positive and negative effects of mediated communication has been the notion of 'reduced social cues'. Studies have shown that information about a person's age, gender, ethnicity and social standing will influence how they are treated in social situations, and how their ideas are received in discussion. CMC strips away these cues, or at least makes them far less prominent, concentrating the attention on the content of the message and the way in which it is expressed. For example, experimental studies of decision making in small-group discussions have shown that the popularity of ideas is strongly influenced by the social standing of the person who first proposes them, and that the higher status members of the group contribute more (in the sense of talking more) in the discussion. Both of these effects are greatly reduced, if not eliminated entirely, when the discussions are conducted through the medium of electronic mail.

Communicating with Technology

Science fiction frequently speculates about the ways in which we would respond to the presence of human-like artificial intelligences. Films like *Bladerunner*, *AI*, *Alien*, or *The Stepford Wives* propose that these technological creations might be physically indistinguishable from other humans, and that it is sometimes very subtle anomalies in behaviour that 'give the game away'. Other fictional characters are quite physically unlike us, and yet appear to have human-like personalities manifest in their behaviour – like the robots R2D2 and C3PO in the *Star Wars* films.

Beyond the realm of science fiction, however, a number of studies have suggested that social psychology has much to say about our uses of, and responses to, the computer technologies that we already find around us today. One prominent group of studies has been carried out by Byron Reeves and Clifford Nass at Stanford University in the USA. In a comprehensive body of research, they and their colleagues have set out to test the hypothesis that predictions from the field of social psychology will hold true when a computer is substituted for a human in a two-way interpersonal interaction. One notable example of this research is based on the idea of 'politeness'. Student participants were asked to work with a piece of computer software for a period of time, with a view to evaluating its usability. They were then asked to respond to a series of questions about their experience. These questions were presented, and their responses recorded, on a computer screen. The experimental manipulation was simple. Either the evaluative questions were presented on the same computer with which they had previously worked or on an identical machine at the other side of the room. The participants rated the software more positively when their answers were given to the same machine than they did when the answers were given to a different machine. What is more, the participants were undergraduates in computer science from one of the most prestigious centres of that discipline in the world, who denied vehemently that their behaviour would be open to manipulation in such a way!

What we can take from such studies, then, is nothing to do with the subtlety of artificial intelligence, but rather the suggestion that humans are strongly inclined to see sociability in the outside world, and that relatively unsophisticated technology can evoke this response from us.

METHODOLOGY OF SOCIAL PSYCHOLOGY

There are a number of ways in which psychologists can gain insights into social processes. The first is simply to watch. Observations of human behaviour in natural settings can provide information about regularities and patterns, such as, for instance, how far apart we normally stand when we talk, or how we use eye contact to signal turn-taking in conversations. This observational approach has been used to investigate so called 'body language', and was popularised thirty years ago by books like Desmond Morris's *Man Watching*. Secondly, experiments can be set up which specifically manipulate the circumstances of social experience to study the consequences of certain circumstances.

Another means by which psychologists can study the products of attempts at social communication is by examining 'text' of various sorts. We put the word in quotation marks here, since it is used in this context to refer not only to pieces of written or spoken language but also to all forms of signs and symbols produced by people with the intention to communicate or influence. The signs in a public building, the packaging on consumer goods, the layout of a church

building or the form of a video game would all be examples
of texts which could be 'read' to gather insights about their
creators' views and understandings of social relationships.
For example, a sign on the table of a college canteen saying
'Reserved for Staff' can tell us something about the social
hierarchy of the organisation. The depiction of men and
women in advertising will tell us something about the social
understanding of gender in relation to the product being
marketed. Written language can obviously be a rich source
of information about the author's view of the social world.
And what does it mean to choose the red pill rather than the
blue one?[1]

This linguistic approach, developing since the 1980s particularly in the UK and Europe, is characterised by a rejection
of the strong reliance on experiment and measurement within
social psychology, and the adoption of a qualitative approach.
This approach is sometimes referred to as Discourse Analysis,
and language has become its central concern. Discourse ana-
lysts do not consider that human social behaviour is best
understood by an approach that seeks to identify and manipulate key variables as in the mainstream experimental psychology tradition. They view our social world as organised by
shared rules and understandings. For example, to understand
what 'Scottish' identity is, it is necessary to examine how
people negotiate, dispute and achieve that identity. This may
be done by both listening to how people talk about it, and
studying how it is written about and reported in the media.

Spears, Holloway and Edwards (2005) provide a clear
account of this approach in an article examining the decon-
struction of newspaper headlines. The headline in question is a
front page story from the *Guardian*, that appeared in May
2004 concerning the inexplicable death of an Iraqi man who
had been detained by the occupation forces. The eye-catching
headline, 'I will always hate you people', came from the wife of
the dead man, who was pictured alongside him, together with
her children. The discourse analyst is interested in the report

---

[1] An allusion to a scene in the film *The Matrix*.

itself rather than the reactions of the readers. Consequently analysis is concerned with how the story is reported, the opportunity created within the story for making a causal explanation and the potential implications for politics and policy. The discourse analyst might be interested in how the use of a direct quotation, as in the headline, impacts, on the reader. What are the general characteristics and uses of direct quotations, and in the performance of what kinds of activities do people produce quotes of what others have said?

We cannot take the interpretation of such texts at face value, however, as we know that social communication has a lot to do with image – the presentation of ourselves to others as we would want them to see us rather than as we really are. The notion of 'how we really are' raises deeply problematic questions for psychologists in many areas of research. Assuming that – given the current state of our technology – we cannot directly know the mind of another person, we are faced with the challenge of arriving at as close an approximation as possible. Rather than attempting to provide you with a shallow resolution of what is a deep and important controversy in psychological research, we will go down a particular route in the knowledge that it will take us directly into the matter of ethics in social research. See how quickly you can spot where we are going.

Many researchers have found that their results depend crucially on what the participants in their studies believe their research is about, and on what the participants think that the researcher expects to happen. People will generally, as far as possible, do what is asked on them, and this holds true in the area of psychological research. If participants believe that they know what the researcher is trying to find, the participants will subconsciously behave in a way that tends to deliver the expected results. Researchers speak of the 'demand characteristics' of a study, referring to this impression that may be conveyed as to what the study is about, or 'the good subject effect', referring to the motivation of the participants to help the researcher out. Indeed, there is a whole field of research into the social psychology of doing social research. (By the way, we have been referring to the 'participants' while talking about the people who become involved in psychological research as the 'subjects of study'. Until recently the term 'subject' was routinely used to refer to these people – as in the 'good subject effect' mentioned above – but the term 'participant' has come to be considered more appropriate, as it has a more collaborative and courteous ring to it. In the spirit of a social psychologist analysing this text, you might like to reflect on the different attitudes that the words 'subject' and 'participant' would convey.)

With this 'good subject effect' in mind, then, it is important that participants in a study remain in ignorance of the aims of that study. Ignorance may not be enough, however, as people will always try to guess what they are not told explicitly. The researcher may have to mislead the participants, giving them some sort of plausible story about the research that is quite unrelated to its real objectives. There is a very fine line between keeping people in ignorance and lying to them, and the ethics of deception in research is a deeply problematic area. Lying can have negative consequences on a number of levels. People can be upset by the nature of the lie, or can feel their self-esteem damaged when it is revealed to them that they have been 'taken in'. Deception in research with children can be particularly damaging, as the child might lose trust in adults, or learn that adults lie when it suits their purposes.

In one famous series of studies conducted by the psychologist Stanley Milgram, people were led to believe that they were participating in a study of the effects of punishment on learning, and were asked to give electric shocks (sometimes at potentially lethal levels) to other participants. The actual objective of the study was to investigate to what extent, and under what circumstances, people would do what they were told by an authority figure. There were, in reality, no shocks, and the person that the participants thought that they were 'punishing' in the learning experiments was actually a confederate of the researcher – an actor instructed to behave in certain ways. To cut a long story short, Milgram's studies demonstrated that many of us would find ourselves behaving in quite barbaric ways, against what would seem to be our own better judgement, when instructed to do so by a malign authority.

Milgram's participants were debriefed after the study, reassured that they had not actually been causing anyone any pain and were introduced to the actor who provided further reassurance. But the experience was clearly an upsetting one for many of them. Think about how you would feel if you believed that you had been prepared to administer electric shocks to someone who, in some of the studies, protested that they had a heart condition! Then consider how you would feel when you learned that the whole business had been an elaborate fabrication. Interestingly, many of the participants claimed that their involvement in the study had given them valuable insights into their own motives, which would help them to recognise and resist malign authority in the future. Milgram claimed that the studies would help us to understand, and thus prevent, the sorts of appalling human rights abuses like those seen during the Holocaust of World War II. A study of this sort could never be carried out under current ethical guidelines.

Our purpose in describing these studies is not to criticise Milgram's ethical position, but rather to highlight the difficulties inherent in conducting research with human participants. Before beginning the studies, Milgram described what he planned to a panel of psychiatrists, asking what would be the psychological impact on those participants who complied with the instructions to shock the confederate. He was told not to worry – there would be no impact!

FURTHER READING

Hayes, Nicky (1993), *Principles of Social Psychology*, Hove: Lawrence Erlbaum Associates.

Manstead, T. and Wetherell, M. (2005), 'Dialoguing across divisions', *The Psychologist*, vol. 18, September, pp. 542–4.

This article, written by two of the UK's leading exponents of Discourse Analysis, introduces a special edition of *The Psychologist* devoted to the different research approaches within social psychology.

Spears, R. Holloway, W. and Edwards, D. (2005), 'Three views on hate', *The Psychologist*, vol. 18, September, pp. 544–7. This article adopts three perspectives – that of the experimentalist, the discourse analyst and the psychoanalyst – to examine a newspaper headline.

9 INDIVIDUAL DIFFERENCES

It is obvious that individuals differ one from the other, but there are patterns which enable us to define dimensions of individual differences. This is the key concern of differential psychology.

One of the growth areas in differential psychology over recent years has been an expansion in the development of selection tests by employers. Known as psychometric testing, this field is concerned with charting how people are similar to or different from one another. The psychometrician aims to measure these individual differences in a reliable and standardised fashion. It is an area of obvious interest to employers seeking to select individuals best fitted for certain kinds of jobs requiring particular talents and aptitudes. Two major areas of interest have been the development of intelligence tests and measures of personality assessment. The field of individual differences extends, moreover, to clinical and abnormal psychology, where there are close connections with the development of theories of personality. Historically, however, psychometrics begins with intelligence testing, and it is this we shall consider first.

INTELLIGENCE AND INTELLIGENCE TESTING

We use the term 'intelligent' readily in our everyday speech, but psychologists are hard pressed to provide an acceptable definition of exactly what the term means. A famous conference in 1921, attended by all the leading scholars of the time, failed to come up with any one agreed definition, and this seems as true today as it was then. The nature of intelligence, and more particularly the field of intelligence testing, have proved to be highly contentious areas of investigation.

Francis Galton (1822–1911), an independently wealthy scientist, developed the first intelligence test, which he administered to over 9,000 people attending the International Health Exhibition in London in 1884. His exhibit, called the Anthropometric Laboratory, was subsequently transferred to the Natural History Museum in South Kensington, where the data collection continued for a period. Galton, a cousin of Charles Darwin, was stimulated by the publication of Darwin's *Origin of Species* and devoted himself to measuring the influence of heredity on the mental and physical characteristics of human beings. His pioneering attempts to measure physical and psychological functions are the start of the scientific study of individual differences.

The French psychologist Alfred Binet (1857–1911) was asked by the French government to devise tests to aid in the selection of children who would benefit from improved secondary education. It is Binet who devised the first formal intelligence test, and who coined the term 'IQ'. Binet ranked various test items on a difficulty dimension, measured by the age at which a particular item was correctly answered by a majority of children. A child would be given a mental age of eight if the score they obtained was typical of an eight-year-old, irrespective of how old the child was at the time of testing. The intelligence quotient, or IQ, is mental age divided by chronological age and multiplied by 100. It was regarded as an indication of the child's performance relative to that of their age group.

Perhaps the most enduring influence in the development of intelligence testing has been the work of Charles Edward Spearman (1863–1946), one of the luminaries of British psychology. Spearman is commemorated by the British Psychological Society to this day through an annual medal in his name, given to a young psychologist who has contributed groundbreaking research in his or her first ten years since graduation. Spearman was a considerable statistician, who developed the technique of factor analysis to analyse the relationships between different kinds of tests. The recipient of the Medal in 2006, Dr Padraig Monaghan of York University, gained his PhD at Edinburgh. Monaghan looked at individual differences in the mental structures and processes involved in students' learning of reasoning.

The technique of factor analysis has been used by other prominent psychometricians interested in intelligence such as Thurstone, Cattell and Eysenck. Spearman's approach involved collecting scores on a large number of tasks that seem to predict intelligent performance, and analysing the patterns of individual differences in test performance. It is this work which resulted in the idea of a general intelligence factor known as g. Spearman examined the correlation between various tests of particular intellectual abilities – spatial, verbal reasoning, arithmetic and so on – and concluded that the modest correlations between scores on different tests was due to g. It would be this factor which might determine how good you are, for example, at analysing the works of Shakespeare. If you scored highly on g you would generally do well on many different kinds of tests, but exceptional performance on some, such as pitch discrimination or painting, is said to be due to specific factors, s. Hence his theory is a two-factor theory of intelligence.

The US psychologist Raymond Cattell (1971) questioned the idea of a single general capacity g, preferring to split this into two differing forms – crystallised and fluid intelligence. Fluid intelligence refers to that measured by relatively culture-free tasks such as Raven's Progressive Matrices, a test that requires one to identify how a series of patterns is progressively changing and to choose, from a set of possible choices, the next pattern in the sequence. This form of intelligence is therefore a measure of our potential ability to learn and solve problems. Crystallised intelligence is a measure of our cultural knowledge and understanding, such as vocabulary and the general knowledge acquired in the course of education.

At the end of the twentieth century two theories advocating multiple intelligences have gained adherents – Howard Gardner's (1983) eight basic forms of intelligence and the more prominent triarchic theory of intelligence of Robert Sternberg (1985). This latter theory advocates three types – analytic, practical and creative intelligence. Analytic intelligence is crucial for good academic performance since it involves the ability to write clearly and to be critical and numerate. Practical intelligence is a kind of procedural intelligence (rather like the notion of procedural memory which we discussed in Chapter 6) and is a measure of our ability to know how to do things, such as strip down and repair an engine or build a dog kennel. Creative intelligence is closely related to Cattell's fluid intelligence and is the ability to formulate novel solutions to problems. Sternberg has published research indicating that education needs to be allied to the strongest form of these three intelligences. In other words, if you have high practical intelligence, you will more easily learn how to build something by undergoing a practical apprenticeship than you will by reading an instruction book. There are interesting parallels here with the idea of different learning styles (see Chapter 10). A further theory which has achieved prominence outside academia has been Daniel Goleman's emotional intelligence (1995). We are all familiar with a situation where someone we recognise to be intelligent behaves in an uncontrolled and counterproductive fashion. They lack the ability to understand emotions and how they impact on others – the capacity which has become known as emotional intelligence.

After reading these few paragraphs you may well believe there are as many different forms of intelligence as there are tests to measure them, and what seems to be lacking here is a theory which tells us what intelligence actually *is*. A task force of the American Psychological Association (Neisser et al. 1996) set out to produce an authoritative statement on what we know of intelligence. One phenomenon it addressed is the extraordinary increase in measured IQ recorded in the western world – a phenomenon named after its discoverer as the Flynn Effect. IQ has had a mean increase of about three points every ten years since the 1930s, although tests are in fact adjusted to keep the mean at 100. The largest gains are in the most culture-free tests such as Raven's matrices (see page 97). The APA report offers three possible explanations for this dramatic rise in IQ. It may be due to better nutrition influencing brain function, in the same way that improved nutrition has resulted in increases in average height. Perhaps the increased challenges of our daily lives compared to previous decades, and the resultant coping with them, has raised IQ. Maybe, alternatively, it is technology which has helped us become more comfortable with abstract thinking – so all those interactive computer games are beneficial after all! This final idea has been the subject of a recent book by Steven Johnson, *All of the Bad Things are Good for You* (2005).

In his book *Looking Down on Human Intelligence* (2000), Professor Ian Deary writes that 'psychometric intelligence is a principal player among one's mental cast'. Deary argues that there can be little doubt of the central importance of a general intelligence factor (Spearman's g) accounting for around 40–50 per cent of the statistical variance in a battery of mental tests administered to a large sample of people. Psychometric intelligence differences show strong stability across the lifespan and are also important predictors of success in both education and the workplace. More surprisingly, recent research shows these differences are also predictive of how long we will live. Deary is excited by the promise of the newer techniques of functional brain imaging and molecular genetics revealing for the first time the true basis of individual differences in the workings of the brain.

PERSONALITY

The concept of personality is based on the observation that people behave consistently over time and across very different situations. Personality traits characterise the individual way of responding to the world around us – the extrovert, for example, seeks out company and enjoys partying, whereas the introvert prefers her own company and avoids overstimulation.

Freud and his influence

Sigmund Freud (1856–1939) the founder of the psychoanalytic movement, is a hugely important figure and arguably the most influential psychologist there has ever been. The influence of his ideas is apparent in literature and biography, in history, in cinema and in our expression of humour. The Freudian theory of personality development and the concepts of repression, fixation and projection are part of our everyday language. You may, however, find that studying Freud is not a major part of your degree course. Why should this be?

Freud was an Austrian physician who became interested in the treatment of patients suffering from hysterical symptoms such as blindness or paralysis, which could appear suddenly and without any obvious physical cause. His detailed clinical observation of individual patients led him to believe that such hysterical symptoms were related to the repression of painful memories and feelings rooted in early childhood experiences, such as sexual abuse. If, under analysis, patients came to relive these repressed memories, then their physical symptoms might disappear or at least show a considerable improvement. This observation convinced Freud of the important role played by the unconscious mind in our waking lives, and he examined the accounts given by patients of their dreams as a means of providing a window on the unconscious mind. His *The Interpretation of Dreams*, published in 1900, is probably his most widely read and important publication.

On the basis of his case studies, Freud divided personality into three separate but interacting structures – the id, the ego and the superego. The id is the most primitive of the three and exists totally within the unconscious mind, having no direct contact with reality. It is the only component present at birth and is the centre of the instinctive psychic energy he called the libido. The id functions in a totally irrational manner according to the pleasure principle (to maximise pleasure and to avoid pain) and seeks immediate gratification. Because the id has no contact with the external world, when the infant reaches between two and three years of age, a new structure emerges, called the ego. The ego functions primarily at a conscious level and operates according to the reality principle. The ego tries to find a realistic and socially acceptable solution to the demands of the id. Finally, the moral component of personality, the superego, emerges between four and six years of age. The superego is our conscience. It is formed as a result of our upbringing, during which we identify with the values of our parents in distinguishing what is right and what is wrong, and it operates according to a morality principle. The superego makes us feel anxious or guilty if we deviate from how we are expected to behave.

The healthy adult personality is a balance between these three structures, which are in a psychodynamic relationship with each other. The ego and the superego both try to control the base instincts of the id. Freud believed that the child goes through a series of psychosexual stages when the id's desire for pleasure is focused on particular erogenous zones of the body. Deprivation or excess can occur at any of the psychosexual stages resulting in fixation, a state of arrested psychosexual development in which the libido becomes focused on a particular region. Babies are constantly exploring the world with their mouths by sucking and mouthing objects. If we become stuck in this oral stage of development, then as adults we are said to be orally fixated. This might manifest itself as smoking cigarettes, nail biting or eating excessively.

Critics of Freud argue that his theories are not scientific since many of their basic tenets are simply untestable, with key concepts not fully defined and their interpretation left open. The theories are complex and can both explain and explain away almost everything – an apparent contradiction within someone's personality, for instance, is justified as due to a defence mechanism. Finally, Freud is criticised because he based his theories on a relatively small sample of mainly upper class women in his native Vienna. These case studies were sometimes written up many years subsequent to the analysis, and therefore subject to all the vagaries and distortions of memory. However, it should be admitted that objections based on cultural specificity can be applied to many areas of psychology. Insights from anthropology and sociology may well be important in developmental and cognitive domains as well as within the field of individual differences.

Personality Traits

The scientific study of personality began in the 1930s with Allport's identification of a basic core of personality traits. These are enduring personal characteristics which predispose us to behave in a particular way in different situations. This pioneering approach was refined by Raymond Cattell, who obtained self-ratings of a number of behavioural characteristics from several thousand people. Cattell then used the statistical technique of factor analysis to identify a smaller number of basic personality dimensions or factors. This resulted in sixteen personality factors and the development of a widely used test known as the 16 PFI. Factors are aspects of the individual that are highly correlated with each other. For example, someone who describes themselves as shy and retiring is also highly likely to say they prefer their own company and to dislike social gatherings – these are behaviours which cluster together. Conversely, people who describe themselves as outgoing and talkative also tend to have lots of friends, enjoy going to parties and prefer not to spend time alone. These two behaviour clusters comprise the personality characteristics of highly introverted and highly extroverted people respectively. These terms, extroversion and introversion derive from the psychoanalyst Carl Jung but are most strongly associated with the eminent British psychologist Hans Eysenck, who died in 1997. Like Cattell, Eysenck used factor analysis to identify key personality dimensions, but reduced the number to only three key factors – extroversion, neuroticism and psychoticism. All are bipolar dimensions in that extraversion is the opposite of introversion, neuroticism is the opposite of emotional stability and psychoticism is the opposite of self-control. At the present time many trait theorists favour the 'Big Five' model of Costa and Macrae (1985): openness, conscientiousness, extroversion, agreeableness and neuroticism – easily remembered by means of the Acronym OCEAN.

THE BROADER CONTEXT

Differential psychology is sometimes associated with a range of highly controversial issues such as the potential differences in mental abilities and personality that might exist between men and women. While such questions may be of intellectual interest, the debates surrounding them often generate more heat than light. There may, however, be important insights to be gained from such perspectives on the increasingly important issue of the underperformance of boys and men in conventional educational systems.

At the extremes of the dimensions used by differential psychology to categorise the normal behavioural spectrum lie those individuals that both science and society would regard as abnormal. Abnormality, from a scientific perspective, may be simply a statistical notion of a state of affairs that is encountered rarely or infrequently. The lay notion of abnormality, on the other hand, directs attention to those individuals whose behaviour is regarded as somehow weird, or which may constitute a danger to themselves or others.

In summary, then, notions of individual difference constitute an area of psychology with considerable applied importance in the world.

FURTHER READING

Davies, M. (2004) 'Personality: two ways of thinking about it', *The Psychologist*, vol. 17, November, 638–41.
This article provides a clear account of the importance of the work of Hans Eysenck in his attempts to provide a synthesis between experimental and correlational approaches in personality research.

Deary, I. J. (2001), *Intelligence: A Very Short Introduction*, Oxford: Oxford University Press.
The book takes readers from no knowledge about the science of human intelligence to a stage where they are able to make

judgements for themselves about some of the key questions about human mental ability differences. Each chapter deals with a central issue that is both scientifically lively and of considerable general interest, and is structured around a diagram which is explained in the course of the chapter. The issues discussed include whether there are several different types of intelligence, whether intelligence differences are caused by genes or the environment, the biological basis of intelligence differences, and whether intelligence declines or increases as we grow older.

Deary, I. J. (2003), 'Ten things I hated about intelligence research', *The Psychologist*, vol. 16, October, pp. 534–7.
This short article is a summary of Professor Deary's book *Looking Down on Intelligence: From psychometrics to the Brain*. OUP, 2000, which was the winner of the British Psychological Society's book award for 2002.

Neisser, J. (1996), The American Psychological Association Intelligence Task Force Report, http://www.indiana.edu/~intell/apa96.shtml
Petridies, K. V., Furnham, A., and Frederickson, N. (2004), 'Emotional Intelligence', *The Psychologist*, vol. 17, October, pp. 574–77.
Despite the concept of emotional intelligence being widely known through the popular success of Daniel Goleman's book, it remains a neglected area in academic research. The authors of this article argue for a trait approach to understanding emotional intelligence.

PART II
The University Experience and Psychology

10   GETTING THE MOST OUT OF LECTURES

The word 'lecture' literally means 'a reading', although your dictionary will tell you that this is an archaic usage. It comes from the Latin *legere*, meaning to read. The origins of the lecture were in a time when books were rare, and the only way that students could obtain access to their contents was to travel to a centre of learning in which books could be found. There they would sit and listen as a particular book was read, doing their best to copy down its contents. This may well suggest to us some of the least positive examples of the lecture experience. You have probably heard the lecture defined as a means of transferring the contents of the notes on the lecturer's bench into the contents of the notes on the student's desk, without it passing through the brains of either. Bad lectures can be dire. But let us return to the earlier historical period with which we began, when the book was a source of some scholar's unique perspective on the world. The lecture, at its best, still provides this source of unique perspective. Lectures should be judged on the basis of what they set out to achieve, and students should try to identify what the lecture is trying to do and to work with those intentions to maximise the benefits from the situation.

WHAT IS THE LECTURER TRYING TO ACHIEVE?

Conveying information to a large audience while trying to cover particular topics and allow students to take effective notes requires careful planning. Here are some of the issues that a lecturer will be trying to achieve in his or her delivery:

- To put across key concepts and cover a particular topic area with a large group of people;

- To put a particular 'spin' on a subject, attempting to make it relevant for a certain course group;

- To set the pace, such that the class are all paying attention to the same issues at the same time, thus providing a common basis for discussion;

- To guide the student in a process of understanding the background controversies associated with these ideas;

- To encourage the student to enquire more deeply through private study by reading from textbooks and original articles;

- To enable the student to think critically about issues.

In addition, the lecturer may sometimes set themselves the task of bringing together ideas from a relatively new area of research for which no good review yet exists. Perhaps the lecturer will talk about information that he or she has heard recently at a scientific conference, or which is just emerging from research that is being carried out in the institution to which you belong. A lecturer may try to emphasise the relevance of a topic by discussing it in the context of a current news story, such as an incident concerning terrorism, child abuse or mental health. Think about the lecture as one person's unique perspective, containing insights that you could not get in another way. Remember too that the lecturer may want you to think about ideas that are not commonly held elsewhere, or which are matters of significant disagreement. Do not expect your lecturers always to agree in every aspect of interpretation with the accounts that you will read in textbooks. Controversy is an important part of scientific advancement.

You will, hopefully, encounter lecturers who really can inspire students, creating an atmosphere of focused and eager attention which may be punctuated by bursts of laughter and even unsolicited questions from the audience. However, these situations are rare, and mostly you may feel your lectures are rather humdrum experiences. But don't forget that learning is a two-way process – yes, you need a guide in the form of a lecture/book/tutorial, but you also need to be engaged with this, which sometimes needs working at. When psychologists have looked at how students learn they make a distinction between deep and surface learning. The former is a more active process on the part of the student: you clarify and supplement your notes by additional reading, you flag up critical points and areas where you may disagree with what has been said and you make links between the content of this lecture and other parts of your course. Surface learning, on the other hand, involves skimming over a topic, memorising the content but without reflection, and taking it all as the gospel truth. Because deep learning engages with your existing long-term memory store you will retain this information, whereas the more shallow learning is easily forgotten.

TAKING NOTES

How is the university lecture likely to differ from your experience of taking notes in class when you were at school? It is likely that you will be expected to be more selective about what you write down rather than trying to record everything as if taking dictation. You may well find yourself in a lecture hall holding several hundred students – not at all untypical of first year classes in psychology. You will find that some students hardly write down anything, while others rarely look up from their notes, so intent are they at capturing everything which is said.

A good lecturer should give you some indication at the start of what they will cover in the next hour, and provide an outline structure. However, whereas at school your peers all had a similar level of knowledge about a subject, now you may find yourself in the company of those for whom the subject matter is completely new and those who may be familiar with the material. In 2004 it was estimated that one in four AS students studied psychology. This may mean that some people in the audience may be taking very few notes while others are scribbling away furiously. And, of course, unlike school the lecturer is unlikely to notice what you are doing amongst so many – whereas your schoolteachers may well have commented on your lack of note-taking, this will not happen at university. You are deemed to be sufficiently motivated to simply get on with the job. It is possible that some individuals can remember everything that has been said without talking any notes – a famous example of such a superior memory is the case of S, a journalist on the Soviet newspaper *Pravda* in the 1920s. It was the practice of the editor to brief the journalists each morning on what their duties were, and he noticed that, unlike the others, S never wrote down any notes at these briefings. When challenged, S astonished the editor by recounting verbatim everything he had said (Luria, 1987)! Your aim should be more to aid your understanding of the material than to recall all the fine detail – this can be checked in a course textbook. So an active strategy might be to write down some of your own ideas and comments on the material given, linking this to knowledge you already have or to other topics in the course which you feel have a similarity or a sharply contrasting view.

Do not think of your notes as a product of the lecture experience, or as a record of the facts that the lecturer was trying to pass on to you to be taken away and memorised. Think of them as part of the process of working towards an understanding of the ideas you are studying. The lecturer's contribution is only part of the story, and your notes will be a more or less accurate record of what was being said. You could think of these notes as a set of hypotheses, to be tested against other sources. Was this really what the lecturer intended me to understand? Is my understanding correct, or as full as it might be? How does this fit with what I thought before I heard the lecture, or with the account of the same topic in my textbook? When one account of the topic seems at odds with another (as will inevitably be your experience, time and time again), how can the discrepancy be understood? Might your initial take on one or other (or both) of the different accounts have to be revised to bring them into closer accord?

Or perhaps there is a piece of the jigsaw missing? Research has shown that even the best sets of notes may record only about one half of what the lecturer had to say. And when you are still unable to make two accounts accord with one another, it is worth remembering that much of our understanding is contested to a greater or lesser extent. There are many areas that we thought that we understood in the past, only to have come to realise that this understanding was incomplete, or fundamentally flawed.

VARIATIONS WITHIN THE LECTURE

In practice, the lecture will be broken up in many different ways. There may, for example, be various visual aids, there may be demonstrations, and the lecturer may ask questions of the audience or ask you to form a 'buzz' group with your neighbours – getting you to discuss an issue raised by the lecturer with, say, the person on your left or either side of you (the 'buzz' refers to the rising level of sound as these conversations get underway). Such techniques not only keep you alert and relieve the monotony of simply listening to the lecturer's voice, but also serve the very useful function of encouraging co-operation and helping you get to know your fellow students. Learning is enhanced when it is more like a team effort than a solo race. Good learning, like good work, is collaborative and social, not competitive and isolated. Working with other students invariably increases involvement in learning. Your own thinking and understanding will be enhanced by sharing ideas with others and, in turn, responding to their reactions.

It is really helpful early in your university career to overcome any nervousness about speaking out in public. Do not worry about your question or answer seeming naive – there will be many others in the audience who have similar views as yourself and they will thank you for speaking out. If you are really unable to speak out during the class, then approach the lecturer at the end of the session when there is often an opportunity to ask questions. Failing this, most lecturers have a class hour when they are available to students with queries about their course. Another increasingly common form of communication is to e-mail the lecturer. Whatever you do, however, try to find out answers for yourself by reading some of the references first. Lecturers are much more likely to respond well to approaches if they feel the student has tried to discover something for themselves. Finally, bear in mind that lecturers like to feel that they have got across the material well to the class and welcome questions – indeed, for lecturers who have allocated a class hour or told students they are happy to respond to queries, there is nothing worse than having no one contact them!

WHAT DOES THE STUDENT WANT FROM THE LECTURE?

The following are some of the most common things students say they are looking for from a lecture:

- Clear. Authoritative and sufficient account of the topic
- Have a good set of notes at the end
- To know what is essential reading and what is icing on the cake
- To have a handout

Almost universal in higher education is the collection of feedback from students about all aspects of their experience, including their lecturers. This can be very useful to the lecturer in gauging how well they have put across their ideas and what they need to do to improve the quality of their teaching. Feedback also highlights the different perceptions of the role of the lecture held by the student and the lecturer. The one thing that feedback and research into student experience in higher education regularly shows is that students greatly value enthusiasm in their lecturers. Some lecturers are natural performers and speakers. Others will be more intro-verted and less demonstrative. Try to see what excites your lecturers, and what issues they find particularly interesting.

HOW THE LECTURE HAS CHANGED OVER THIRTY YEARS

If your parents had some form of higher education when they were your age, their lectures would have been largely black-board-and-chalk affairs, with relatively little in the way of audiovisual aids. Today, at the very least, you will find exten-sive use of slide projectors and overheads for showing figures, photographs and illustrations, and you will also be shown videos. Such aids can be managed by software tools, and many lecture halls will have computer provision for this purpose. These additions can enormously enhance the power of the lec-turer to involve the audience, but they are only tools and the real skill rests with the ability of the lecturer to present the material well. You should therefore be prepared for consider-able differences in style from the traditional 'chalk and talk' to the high-tech multimedia presentation.

What about the future? Many educationists are now con-vinced that the lecture format is outdated, and that the future lies with 'problem-based learning', now adopted in the more innovative medical schools. The basis for this approach lies in sound psychological theory – the pioneering work of Jean Piaget for example – and its time may well have arrived as children grow up very used to the idea of accessing informa-tion via the internet. The approach involves students being presented with a problem and asked to find out as much as they can from any available source, rather than having the facts presented to them. Research suggests that students who have experienced this form of teaching may know fewer facts than those who experience conventional lectures, but they are more satisfied and motivated by their education and, most importantly, are much better prepared for future learning.

PHENOMENOLOGICAL DEMONSTRATIONS IN PSYCHOLOGY

The subject matter of psychology is an understanding of the human mind, and very often the best way to develop such understanding is to get everyone to participate in and experience the issue at hand. This might involve a demonstration of the blind spot in the eye by asking students to draw and view a diagram (see Chapter 5); to participate in a data collection exercise in the class to illustrate the nature of sex differences in behaviour (see Chapter 8); or to learn a short list of words to demonstrate important distinctions between different forms of memory (see Chapter 6). Psychology lends itself very well to these kinds of exercise, and the involvement they call for means that the memory persists and extends to other material in that same session. Perhaps you may experience a practical example of the failings of memory in an eyewitness testimony demonstration. This was first tried at a college in North America, where unknown to the audience a student actor was present. Some way into the lecture this person created a disturbance, shouting, clambering over the lecture seats before leaving the room. This drew the attention of the class to the person, and in the next lecture the students were asked to describe as accurately as they could the clothing and appearance of the actor. Subsequent presentation to the students of a photograph of the actor, or having him reappear dressed as he was previously, is a convincing demonstration of the fallibility of this form of memory recall.

Finally, we must stress that lectures only provide a framework of the topic under consideration, which you have to flesh out by adding to your own notes after consulting the course textbooks. As you progress in your studies this will mean seeking out original source material – looking up journal articles and evaluating the evidence in support of a theory or criticism of an existing experiment. Try to do this kind of reading close in time to the lectures, rather than leaving it all until just before the exams. It will not only make your revision more manageable, but enable you to clarify aspects you do not understand directly with the lecturer soon after the topic has been discussed.

FURTHER READING

Crook C. (2004), 'Ripe for a Virtual Revolution?', *The Psychologist*, vol 17, April, pp. 202–04.
Charles Crook is at the University of Nottingham. This thoughtful account examines the changes in higher education with the advent of e-learning and virtual environments, concluding that conventional education may work precisely because it employs the convivial modes of communication characteristic of everyday life.

Luria, A. R. (1987), *The Mind of a Mnemonist*, London: Harvard University Press.
This classic account of a man with an exceptional memory is an example of the honourable tradition of individual case histories in psychology. Luria was a leading Russian neuropsychologist and here gives a very human account of the plight of someone who quite literally could forget nothing. In this second edition to the original, first published in 1967, there is an illuminating introduction by another eminent psychologist and educationist, Jerome Bruner. Bruner describes the book as being in the spirit of Kafka or Beckett, both of whom wrote about characters who are symbolically dispossessed of the power to find meaning in the world.

Schwartz, S. (2004), 'Time to bid goodbye to the psychology lecture', *The Psychologist*, vol. 17, January, pp. 26–27.
In this article Steven Schwartz, professor of psychology at Brunel University, describes the nature of problem-based learning in medical schools and argues for its introduction into psychology teaching.

11 LEARNING IN SMALL GROUPS

*Education is what remains after one has forgotten
everything he learned in school.*

Albert Einstein

While the whole group of students with whom you will be
studying is likely to be quite large (perhaps numbering several
hundred), you will most likely find that your timetable will
contain some classes that are divided into smaller groups. In
contrast to a large lecture meeting, the small group tutorial or
seminar class may feel more familiar to you, reminiscent of a
class at school. In fact, very few students will have experienced this form of teaching and learning when at school, and
so expectations can be very diverse.

LEARNING OPPORTUNITIES

The essence of a university education should be the exchange
of ideas, and it is in the seminar and in the tutorial where you
will hopefully experience this form of learning. We quite delib-
erately use the word 'learning' rather than 'teaching' here, as
it is up to you to make the most of this experience, and not to
adopt an essentially passive mode with the expectation that
the tutor will give you a mini-lecture. We saw in Chapter 10
that this traditional form of oration centres on the lecturer, and
we can contrast this with the tutorial, where the students
should be the major contributors to the discussion. There are
clearly two perspectives here. Tutors look to the students to
take the lead, and see their role as essentially that of facilita-
tor, while students encounter the tutorial as another form of
instruction, albeit in a different format from the lecture.

Most degree courses will include an element of tutorial work. Individual or shared tutorials with two or three other students, although still present in collegiate universities such as Oxford and Cambridge are the exception rather than the rule. The size of the tutorial will depend very much on the popularity of and overall numbers in the course. Since psychology is generally a very popular subject, you may find first-year groups typically have between ten and twenty students, and will meet on a weekly or fortnightly basis. Your tutor may be a member of the lecturing team for the psychology course, or, as is typical in large universities with a substantive research agenda, a postgraduate student. Postgraduate students will themselves be working towards a higher degree (a Masters or Doctoral degree), having already completed their own undergraduate studies. This will involve them primarily in carrying out their own original research, making them extremely knowledgeable in their own small area of concern. They will most likely have first degrees in psychology, but sometimes they will have come to research in psychology from another area, like neuroscience or mathematics.

Remember that the purpose of the tutorial is not simply to 'instruct' you. The tutorial is not just another form of lecture, intended to convey information. For example, if the tutor asks the group to tell him or her about the content of a recent lecture, the intention is not to find out how much you remember and somehow 'fill in the blanks'. A question of this sort will be directed towards getting you to think about what was raised in the lecture, what you understood from what was being said, and what questions it raised for you. There is no need therefore for the tutor to be intimately familiar with the lecture content. He or she will be able to help you to develop your own understanding without having that detailed knowledge. When a tutor asks you a question it will not be directed towards assessing how much you know or remember, but rather as a means of getting you to come out with your own ideas. Graduate students are certainly not 'second-best' tutors – they are strongly motivated to be seen as good teachers, and will consequently put a great deal of effort into their teaching. Their similarity in age and experience to undergraduate students can be a real advantage – they are familiar with the anxieties of students, since they were in that same position themselves a few years earlier. There is also evidence that postgraduate tutors are more effective than academic staff at facilitating productive interactions in small groups (Howe, 2004).

Seminars usually take place in the later years of a course, and are more likely within a specialist option rather than in large introductory classes. Here, the emphasis is much more on the in-depth discussion of a particular book or journal article, and will often consist of one or more students presenting a short critical account of the material they have been reading. In other words, not only will you be expected to take an active role as in the tutorial setting, but you will also be called upon to lead discussions based upon a significant amount of preparation. For the purposes of discussing the dynamics of small-group teaching, however, we will focus on tutorials and not seminars as the former will be your most likely first encounter with such teaching.

DIFFERING VIEWS OF SMALL-GROUP TEACHING

A good deal of research has been conducted into the various teaching methods in higher education. One issue it has highlighted regarding small-group teaching is that 'it depends as much on student training as on teacher training'. When students are asked for feedback on university courses they invariably say they want more small-group teaching, but in practice the tutorial can often degenerate into a mini-lecture with the tutor talking for most of the contact time and the students adopting a passive listening mode. There is definitely a tension here for tutors. It is generally true that students want to be told things and expect tutors to know all the answers, while tutors want to encourage them to think for themselves. How do the students perceive the tutor, and how does the tutor interpret the behaviour of the students? The relationship between the tutor and the students is crucial, as is an agreed understanding from both sides as to what the tutorial is for. Students may want to be told things about the topic of study, and find the tutor unhelpful if he or she does not conform to that expectation. The tutor, on the other hand, may attribute a student's reluctance to talk in a tutorial to laziness or lack of interest, while the problem is really uncertainty on the part of the student about what is wanted.

It is quite instructive to look at the comments that both tutors and students make about small-group teaching. The following examples are taken from a doctoral dissertation by Luker (1987) into case studies of small-group teaching, reported in Brown and Atkins (1988). When asked to list what they enjoyed most about small-group teaching, tutors said:

> *The informal atmosphere – an opportunity to get to know students at a personal level and for them to get to know me.*

> *I can be stimulated by student 'ideas'.*

> *Feelings of informality, and when things go right, that students have learnt something and – even in Statistics – enjoyed themselves.*

And the students said:

> *I personally have a greater influence on what is being discussed. I can actually remember, and feel I understand what we are discussing.*

> *You can discuss issues together rather than be told them.*

> *By being in a smaller group, one feels part of the class rather than just another face in a sea of faces. I actually feel more part of the university.*

When asked about what they found problematic about the small-group setting, the tutors commented:

Keeping my mouth shut.

Getting students to see me as an equal, to talk to me as they would to their peers, and to lose their inhibitions about displaying ignorance in front of me and their peers.

Very difficult to establish the kind of atmosphere in which students will begin to talk. They tend to be very much afraid of not saying the right thing.

While the students cited as dislikes:

Being asked to contribute when you don't want to.

Long silences.

A feeling of being assessed by the lecturer through your answers to questions and your attitudes.

We therefore have a problem. The tutor will generally find it easy to talk, while the students will, initially at least, find it hard. But the tutor knows, and the students must come to realise, that the tutorial will be most successful when the students say most and the tutor says least.

When one of the authors of this book was of an age when it was possible to be mistaken for a student, he tried the rather daunting experiment of not revealing his role as tutor. He arrived a few minutes before the appointed hour, hoping that some other students were already present, and sat down at the table. Gradually the seats filled up, until all the group members had arrived. As the minutes ticked by, there was an air of restlessness and someone wondered out loud why the tutor had not turned up. One or two others looked at their tutorial sheets, which happened to list the names of all the students and that of the tutor; another suggested that they should go round the table introducing themselves. When it came to the tutor, he revealed his name and that he was, indeed, the tutor. This prompted a puzzled silence and inevitable nervousness from the others, but eventually the tutor said that he was interested to hear from them what they wanted to happen for the next hour. This exercise could have been an abysmal failure, but what actually resulted was a highly informative exchange of views which set the scene for subsequent tutorials. Working out an agenda for operating tutorials should be a joint venture, with the tutor risking as much as the students in either succeeding or failing to put across their viewpoint.

OWNERSHIP OF THE GROUP

To create a successful environment in which to learn, it is important that individuals feel a sense of ownership and therefore responsibility to make the tutorial work. First sessions could involve the tutor in asking students to introduce themselves – perhaps indicating what other subjects they are taking and why they chose psychology. This kind of 'round-robin' exercise will invariably develop a standard pattern of response, with each person following the same format as their predecessors. What do you think might happen if, instead of requiring an oral response, the tutor had asked the students to write down their introductions? This is likely to produce a much more varied response from the students and is a good demonstration of a powerful influence on our behaviour in groups known as social conformity (see Chapter 8). Very likely the written responses would be a more accurate reflection of individual motivations. As psychologists we are in the business of understanding and measuring behaviour, and we need to ask ourselves what influences are at play here. Is personality important – are certain individuals less susceptible to such group pressure? Can we introduce a task in a way which will maximise the chances of getting truthful responses from people?

As a member of the group, you will need to ask yourself what skills you can develop in that situation. It is important to remember that groups have their own dynamics and have been a fertile ground for research in social psychology. The processes of establishing group cohesion, challenging authority and resolving conflict are common to the university tutorial, to society committees and to the boardroom (Argyle 1983). The variables which influence the group dynamic range from the seating arrangements – everyone in a circle, the tutor changing position each time the group meets to encourages exchanges between the students and with the tutor – to the experience of the tutor in paying attention to the shared needs of the group. It can be a very useful exercise to get everyone (including the tutor) to write down what they want to see happening in the group, and to ask how they would like to see themselves change in the course of their meetings. There are no 'right' and 'wrong' answers here, and it can take courage to admit that you are frightened to speak out in the group or that you are worried at seeming ignorant and not understanding what has been discussed. But this is the whole point of the tutorial, to bring together the shared experiences of people thinking about the same topic, even when they hold seemingly incompatible views. This may well be the case comparing the tutor's view of a successful tutorial ('I hardly spoke, the students engaged in a lively discussion; there was a fierce exchange of views; there was evidence of people changing their minds having heard and discussed the evidence') and the student's ('I wasn't required to say anything; the tutor gave us a handout covering the topic; he told us we did not need to bother reading all the references on the reading list as these were all covered in the main textbook').

It will be obvious from what has gone before that a successful tutorial calls for a significant degree of trust and respect among the members of the group. It is the nature of psychology that people will hold strong views about much of what will be discussed, and those views may not always be in agreement. In a tutorial you should feel able to speak openly about what you think, but you should do so in a way which is sensitive and which attempts not to give offence. If you hear something that appears to contradict a belief or understanding that is important to you, you must strive not to take offence but to express your opposing view in a way that does not attribute ill intent to the other person. Discussion involves lots of interpersonal skills that you will have to work to develop, and the tutorial experience and your tutors should help you to do that.

You could try writing a list of goals you would like to achieve in the course of the sessions. For instance:

I would like to be more interested in the subject.
I want to express my opinions clearly in the group.
I want to be able to ask questions about things I do not understand.
I want to find out how the mark awarded for my work could be improved upon.

You could also formulate these aims as questions about how you are at the moment, with a rating scale running from 'not at all' to 'very much so'. Completing the same ratings at the end of the course will enable you to see how much of a change you have achieved in this time.

Another way to get the most from tutorials is to consider them as a whole, including the strengths and weaknesses of all of its members and the particular contributions that you have to make. A vibrant discussion needs all sorts of input to make it work. Some people are good at stimulating discussion, and driving the conversation forward. Others are good at summarising and drawing conclusions, or at challenging assumptions that need to be opened out and examined. Some people are good when it comes to easing and resolving conflicts. All these varied contributions are necessary, and you should try to be alert to when each type is needed.

You may find it useful to identify someone who has skills that you would like to acquire, and to observe their behaviour, trying to use the same techniques they have successfully employed. Above all, try to conquer the British disease of praising the amateur at the expense of the professional. These skills are not a question of one-upmanship within the group, they are essential tools for expressing yourself and making your opinions known. They will stand you in very good stead when you eventually encounter the job market, where the detail of what you have learnt from psychology may be of little value, but the skills acquired will be at a premium. The subject matter of the course is only part (and perhaps not the most enduring part) of what you will learn from your experience of your tutorial classes. You will also learn habits of thought and argument which will be of significant use in many areas of your life.

Establishing a good rapport with another tutee will be helpful to both of you as you tackle the course and discuss the reading and preparation for the tutorial together. This also applies to the coursework you will be asked to produce. Try asking a friend to read your essay and give you some feedback on this. Is it well organised? Do they understand all the points you raised? Ideally, this should be a reciprocal exchange.

Your tutor is very likely to provide an e-mail address for any queries you may have – do make use of this, and at an early stage in the course rather than the day before the final exam! Tutors take e-mails as a sign of positive interest in the tutorial material and find them reinforcing rather than an extra work detail. But do remember to try and find things out for yourself as a first step – firing off questions, the answers to which are present in the standard introductory texts, may well receive a dusty answer. Most introductory courses will have an element of coursework – perhaps two or three essays – which will be marked by your tutor. It is often the case that coursework is anonymously marked, but there are real advantages in knowing your tutor, which the informality of the small group can foster. So take this opportunity to engage with him or her to take in fully the feedback that will be provided with your written work.

A final form of group work that you may be offered – the likelihood of this increasing as your studies progress – is the opportunity to work with other students on a data collection exercise involving the design of an experiment or a questionnaire. This ideally can be introduced as problem-based learning (see Chapter 10), where the group is presented with a task and must use their shared skills to set up and carry out a study to elucidate this.

FURTHER READING

Argyle, M. (1970), *The Psychology of Interpersonal Behaviour*, London: penguin.

Brown, G. and Atkins, M. (1988), *Effective Teaching in Higher Education*, London Routledge.

Howe, C. (2004), 'All together Now', *The Psychologist*, vol. 17, April, pp. 199–201.

Based at Strathclyde University, Professor Howe has researched peer learning in young children and students for many years. In this article she looks at what psychological theory and research can teach us about the effectiveness of group work in the undergraduate curriculum.

12 WRITING TO BE READ

The emphasis in the title of this chapter may seem strange to you – of course you expect your writing to be read by someone. We find, however, that lack of clarity about the audience for one's work can be one of the biggest problems facing students in their writing. Very often students write as if the objective of the task – and therefore, by implication, what will earn them good grades – is to demonstrate how much they know about a given topic. We would like to encourage you to see your writing as a communicative act designed to inform, enlighten and persuade.

First of all, what sorts of writing tasks will you be faced with on an undergraduate psychology programme? Some will be reports of your research work, and we deal further with this sort of writing in Chapter 3. You may have to write something that you will read aloud in a seminar or tutorial class, and we mention this sort of written preparation in Chapter 11. The rest of your writing will be of the 'essay' form with which you will probably be most familiar from your secondary school experience. It is this form of writing that we address most particularly here. Essays are frequently referred to as 'papers' in the university setting, suggesting that the student should ultimately aspire to writing something of the format and quality of a paper published in an academic journal.

It is this sort of writing task that can often seem most nebulous and ill-defined in the minds of students, problems that often focus on a lack of clarity about just what one is trying to do. The task will begin with some sort of question, and the job for the student will be to decide what would constitute an appropriate answer, and how that answer should be set out and structured. We believe that keeping an idea of audience in your mind will provide you with a vital basis for your decisions on how to approach the writing, and will also motivate you as you write.

Consider the two essay questions below:

1. *Discuss the contention that video games have negative social and psychological effects on young people.*

2. *The management committee of a local youth club is being lobbied by concerned parents to remove video games from the activities that the club offers to its young members. The parents believe these games have negative social and psychological effects. You have been asked by the management committee (made up of local community professionals and parents' representatives, none of whom have any background in psychology) to write a report that will help them to come to a decision, and provide them with valid evidence to present to the parents in support of the decision that they make.*

We would like to make two claims here. The first is that these two questions are exactly the same from an intellectual point of view, and that a good answer to the first would constitute a good answer to the second. Our second claim is that, had you been given only the second of these questions, you would have felt more comfortable with it, had a clearer idea of how you were going to address it and (dare we suggest?) would have enjoyed writing it more. Studies in cognitive psychology tell us that context is all important when we are thinking about a problem. Something that appears impossibly challenging when posed in the abstract can be much more easily solved when presented in a concrete context.

You will no doubt encounter essay questions that conform to both of these styles. When the question is posed in the more abstract style, should you make up a 'back story' to help you think about the question? The answer to that is, if it helps, then you should do it. But be careful not to let your imaginary context 'leak' into your writing. That said, of course, an appropriately professional report produced in response to the request described in the second essay question above would be written in an objective style that would rarely, if ever, need to make explicit reference to the setting from which the request came.

STRUCTURING AN ESSAY

The old joke has some truth to it: in an essay you should tell them what you are going to say, say it, then tell them what you said. Put more seriously, an essay will most likely be made up of an introduction, the main body of evidence and argument, and finally a statement of what has been concluded. It follows from this that the best way to write an essay is not to start at the beginning and work through to the end. What you say in your introduction will depend, to some degree at least, on what you choose to include in the main body of the work.

In addition to these three broad sections an essay should also contain a reference section (which we will come to in due course) and have a title. The title is an important element, and not simply an afterthought. Some students merely put the essay question in quotation marks at the top, and let this pass for a title. This is not playing the game. The title should serve as a succinct statement of what your essay (as opposed to that of anyone else in the class who chose to address this question) will be about, and may give some indication of any particular emphasis you have chosen to take. Considering again the example above, essay question (1) might produce a range of different titles:

Video games in youth culture: the social and cognitive impact.

Psychological and social influences of young people's engagement with video games.

Themes of aggression and gender stereotyping in video game narratives, and their potential psychological effects.

The introductory section of the essay should set the scene. It might explain why the particular topic at issue is intellectually interesting or socially significant. It might also say something about the history of the development of the ideas to be discussed, or the different traditions within psychology that have addressed the topic. In addition the introduction should provide some overview of the territory your essay is going to cover, and what it intends to achieve.

The main body of your essay should present the evidence and information that you want to call upon, and link these items of evidence together in a logical way. The evidence you will use is likely to be taken from existing published research studies. One format would be to present research which seems to point to one particular conclusion, then follow this with other evidence leading in an alternative direction. Depending on your background of school subjects, you may feel more or less comfortable about using section and subsection headings to provide structure to your essay. In general we would recommend it. Sectioning a piece of writing helps you keep an overview of the whole work, enabling you to see where something is missing or where content might be ordered in a better way. The structure provided by section headings also helps the reader to see where your argument is going. Consider too where summary tables, lists and diagrams might be the best way to communicate an idea.

The concluding section of the essay should set out what you take the evidence you have presented to mean, and any practical or theoretical implications that arise from this. Take care to make your conclusions explicit. Evidence rarely 'speaks for itself', but is open to a range of interpretations. If you have been thinking and reading in a particular area for some time you may be so steeped in the material that you believe the conclusions are obvious. This may not be at all the case for your reader, coming fresh to the topic.

QUALITY CONTROL

Spelling and grammar are important aspects of the quality of your writing. There is sometimes a feeling among students that it should be the factual content of a piece of writing work which is important, and that issues of presentation take second place. This is a false distinction to try to make. Remember that communicative clarity and accuracy are crucial. The aim is to write so that your text is easy to understand and follow, and badly formed sentences and inaccurate spelling distract the reader and detract from communicative success. You should remember too that a poorly presented piece of work may very likely be perceived as somewhat discourteous by the person who has to read it. The impression that you risk giving is that you simply didn't care enough about the work to make the effort to proof-read it thoroughly, which will almost certainly lead to a negative view of the writer, and to a poorer grade than you might otherwise have been awarded.

Dealing with spelling is relatively easy these days. You should be word processing your written work, and therefore you will be able to make use of the spellchecking system which is a component of word processing software. One of the authors of this book is mildly dyslexic and a terrible speller, so we have a great deal of sympathy for those who find spelling difficult. But sophisticated software can help us a great deal. It is particularly important to spell technical words accurately, because the meaning of what is being said will be lost if the wrong word is used. You won't get very far talking about 'social constructionism' when you should be talking about 'social constructivism'.

Grammar and style are somewhat more difficult. Some word processing packages have a 'grammar checking' facility, but this is seldom powerful enough to give you very much help. To judge whether a piece of writing reads well, there is really no substitute for a careful rereading of the text. If you can, finish your writing well before the due date for submission, and then leave the paper for a few days before you attempt to reread it. That way, you will have forgotten just what you said. Reread your paper too soon after having written it and there is a strong tendency for you to read what you know that you intended to write rather than what you actually wrote. Better still, get a student colleague to read the paper for you, and flag up any difficulties. You can perform the same service for him or her on another occasion. Someone other than the author is going to be better placed to spot any errors or problems with the writing.

Even if you are confident about your spelling and grammar you should still get into the habit of asking a student colleague to read and comment on your work. Ask them whether they can understand what you have written, and whether the argument in your paper flows logically. Again, this is something that a group of trusted friends can do for one another. The ability to comment critically on someone else's work is an important skill well worth cultivating. Students often find this very difficult, as we are all disinclined to make negative observations about the work of others. What is wanted, of course, is constructive criticism. It is important to express criticism in a positive and helpful way. Hearing from someone else about the strengths and weakness in how you have expressed yourself can really help you to improve your academic writing. Taking onboard other people's advice in this way should not be regarded as 'cheating'. The ability to seek help at appropriate times, and to respond to the advice that is given, are important academic skills.

Ultimately you will receive constructive criticism from your tutor, and this may be associated with the award of a grade for your work. Make use of this feedback; there is evidence that students frequently do not, focusing rather on the grade. Your tutor's comments will help you to identify strengths and weaknesses in your work, and to improve the next time around.

PLAGIARISM

As we are talking about the help that you can usefully and legitimately receive from others, we should perhaps say something about what are unacceptable ways to use other people's work. Plagiarism can be defined as passing off the work of others as your own. What we were talking about before was asking someone else to read and help you improve your own work. What is unacceptable is to take the writing of someone else, whether that of another student or something taken from a textbook, journal article or website, and incorporate it into your own work without due acknowledgement. Here the work and effort are not yours. The writing belonged first to someone else, and you have misappropriated it for your own gain.

We should point out, however, that we believe that most instances of plagiarism in students' work are based on misunderstanding of the conventions of academic writing rather than on any cynical intent to cheat and mislead. Of course, there are some people who try to copy large chunks of information they have found on the internet, cobble them together and submit the final assembly as their own work. Don't do it. You will be caught: such 'patchwork' plagiarism is easy to spot. Most academic institutions regard this as an extremely serious crime, and penalties are correspondingly severe. Importantly, you are also denying yourself an opportunity to learn.

Much academic writing builds on the work of others, and students at first see a very fine line between creating a synthesis from a number of sources and merely copying from those same sources. We would suggest that there are two key things that you should remember. First of all, you must acknowledge your sources. A direct quotation should be set out as such, with a clear indication of the work from which it came. Where an idea has come from the work of another – even when you are not using a word-for-word quotation – you must also name the source. References should be provided in your work (see below) so that the reader is able to find the sources that you have used. The second point is that your writing should 'add value' to the sources that you have used. By this we mean that you should not merely be reiterating what others have said, but that you should be saying something new and original of your own. That may sound like a very great demand to make of a first year undergraduate! We do not mean that you have to come up with ideas that nobody has ever had before, but that you should draw conclusions of your own that are new and creative for yourself. If you draw two separate pieces of information together there is a creative act in making that link. Explain to your reader why it is useful to see these two ideas joined, and what you conclude from setting them side by side.

PROVIDING REFERENCES

As mentioned above, all of the sources that you rely upon in the construction of your own writing should be suitably acknowledged in your text, and a complete reference to that source provided so that your reader will be able to find it for themselves. There are several different conventions for the setting out of references, and you should be told which you are to use on your courses. And you should not be too surprised if different courses in different subject disciplines ask you to use different conventions. Different traditions exist, frustrating as this may seem. The most common format is the so-called Harvard System, which involves giving the author's name and the date of publication in the body of your text where you use it, and then including the complete reference to the work in an alphabetically ordered list at the end of your paper. For example, if we were to say that Stella Cottrell provides more details of how to set out references in her book on study skills (Cottrell, 2003), we would then include the complete reference to the work in a list at the end, set out as follows:

Cottrell, S. (2003), *The Study Skills Handbook*, Basingstoke: Palgrave Macmillan.

The format is the surname of the author followed by their initials, the year of publication, the title of the book, its place of publication and the name of the publisher. Everything, in short, that would be needed to unambiguously identify the work and find it in a library or bookshop. Every source mentioned in the body of your text should have a corresponding entry in your reference section.

Missing or wrongly constructed reference sections are a great source of annoyance and frustration for tutors. Firstly, because getting it right is such a simple matter – just follow a set of rules and there you are. There is no thought or judgement involved. Not making a decent stab at the reference section will leave a tutor feeling that you are taking your work less than seriously, which they may interpret as a matter of discourtesy. Secondly, it is deeply frustrating to find an essay referring to an interesting piece of work that one has not previously come across, only to turn to the reference section to find that the reference is missing or not sufficiently described to locate the original source. Remember that your tutors (in their better moments at least!) will see you as junior colleagues who will contribute to their understanding of the topic, just as they seek to contribute to yours. That expectation will, of course, increase as you progress through your undergraduate years.

Collecting References

It is never too soon to begin to build up your own collection of useful references. As you read textbooks, academic and popular articles, newspapers and web pages you will find items that you find useful and might want to retrieve later. You should begin from the start to file these away for future reference. There are various manual ways of doing this, such as index cards or an alphabetically structured notebook, but by far the best approach is to use a computerised bibliographic database that can be searched easily for keywords, text or names. Your institution will no doubt have a recommended piece of software available on its machines, and you may be able to obtain a licensed copy for your own computer.

CONCLUSION

Think of your writing as a communicative exchange with another person, or a number of other people. This will help to increase your motivation for the task and improve the clarity of your writing. Seek advice and feedback from peers and tutors, and try to take this onboard in your next assignments. Finally, remember that the acknowledgement of sources is a key aspect of the academic rigour you are working to develop.

FURTHER READING

Sternberg, J. Robert (2003, 4th edition), *The Psychologist's Companion*, Cambridge: Cambridge University Press.
See the remarks made about this useful book on page 12.

In addition, there are many websites which will provide useful hints on writing essays. Be sure, too, to see what is on offer from your own institution by way of workshops on all aspects of assessment and creativity.

13 ONLINE LEARNING

In 1977, at the beginning of the personal computer revolution, Ken Olson, then president of the large computer manufacturer Digital Equipment Corporation, famously observed that 'There is no reason for any individual to have a computer in their home.' This now seems like a remarkable failure of vision. However, the truth of the matter was that he was right. The computer, as conceived at that time, was of little use to the average individual. Computers have clearly increased massively in power since that time, but the major development that made computers into the ubiquitous household appliances that they are today was the widespread access to the internet that took off in the UK in 1994. It has been this convergence of computing technologies with network technologies that has really turned the computer into a powerful personal tool, and is the basis of its widespread use in educational settings. Computers, and their associated networks, give us access to information and to other people, and these are the key resources that support the educational process.

TERMINOLOGY

Any new area of activity requires that we come up with new words and terms to describe what we are doing. The use of technology in teaching and learning is no exception. The words themselves are not important, save that we need to be able to understand what people are talking about. What is really important is what the technology enables us to do. Some of the accounts make it sound as if technology is utterly changing the nature of university education, while others suggest that it is just a matter of doing familiar things in new ways. There is something to be said for both these accounts, and the truth, as always, lies somewhere in the middle.

An early term in this field of technology and education was CAL, standing for computer-aided learning (or perhaps computer-assisted learning). While this term is still quite descriptive it is less used now, having been superseded by online learning, or e-learning. The term 'online learning' serves to emphasise the involvement of networks, while 'e-learning' is derived from the fashion for sticking 'e' in front of words (like e-commerce, or e-government) to denote the involvement of technologies. The term 'e-learning' can be quite useful, as it covers a wide range of uses and influences of technology in education without being too specific about details. We will stick, however, with online learning, and contract it to OLL for convenience.

Another contraction you will encounter is ICT (or sometimes C&IT), standing for information and communication technologies. It is often used in the context of generic ICT skills, as opposed to the specific uses of ICT in teaching and learning. Before it is possible to make significant use of ICT for educational purposes, it is necessary for teachers and students alike to be comfortable with the technologies themselves. Arguably this is less of an issue now than it was a few years ago (although we will return to what might be meant by ICT literacy), with people tending to assume that the basic skills are there, and that what we need to develop is the application of the skills in the learning context.

Another aspect of our use of language in relation to OLL is the widespread employment of metaphor to describe resources and activities. Metaphors help us to understand something new in terms of something with which we are already familiar. Hence passing messages around a group by networked means is a bit like a 'discussion', while accessing large collections of textual materials online can be talked about as 'entering' a 'virtual library'. These metaphors enable us to create mental models, or pictures in our minds, of what is going on, which help our understanding of a task. In some senses, however, an electronic discussion is nothing like a conversation around a table during a conventional tutorial meeting – metaphors can be both a help and a hindrance.

WHAT IS ONLINE LEARNING?

One could define OLL crudely as any application of ICT in a teaching and learning setting, but it could be argued that there is little that one does at university today that does not involve some element of technology. Rather than try for an exhaustive definition, the rest of this chapter describes some examples of what we consider to be OLL. We emphasise what the use of the technology particularly contributes to the learning situation, and how you should approach that situation to gain the most benefit. We start with some examples of ICT use with which you will most likely be familiar, before mentioning some uses that you may not have come across before.

A word of caution first of all, however. Our experience is that most students arrive at university with plenty of experience and confidence in the use of ICT. If this isn't true of you, be assured that there will be general help and support available, and specific instruction when required. But if you are already quite confident in your ability to use certain ICT tools, don't let that blind you to the intellectual challenge of the tasks that you will be set, and the volume of resources that will be made available to you as a member of a university community. We will start by referring to the use of the World Wide Web to emphasise the fact that OLL may involve you in learning to use familiar tools in quite different ways.

THE WORLD WIDE WEB

Most people will have had some experience of using a Web browser, such as Netscape or Internet Explorer, to search for information on the World Wide Web (the Web). Beyond that, you may have used the Web for shopping, to buy travel tickets, to access your electronic mail or to communicate with friends and family through an instant messaging system. Increasingly, a Web browser will be the common route to accessing information online, and you will make routine use of the Web in your studies and research.

The Web browser allows you, sitting at your own computer, to make requests for information from a vast array of other computers all over the world connected to the internet. The way in which information is requested and delivered by the Web can make the whole business feel quite seamless – as if all this information was really contained within the machine on your desk.

When you are set research tasks on your courses, for a piece of writing or preparation for a tutorial or seminar, the Web has become a natural resource to turn to, alongside text-books and journal articles. You should not feel at all reluctant to use standard search sites on the Web (like Google or Yahoo), but you should remember first of all that what you find by this means will not be 'quality controlled' in any way, and you will be responsible for judging its accuracy and authenticity. Furthermore, because you are a member of a university, you will have right of access to databases of academic information – for which your university library will have paid considerable sums of money – that cannot be accessed by the general public. These may include the full texts of journal articles, along with specialist resources like maps, pictures, chemical formulae and structures. Your university library will help you to access these resources. You should find out about them early and use them routinely – they will take you further and faster than the publicly available search tools.

You will also find specialist 'portals' on the Web that will direct you to resources, organised under certain headings that have, to some extent, been subjected to a quality control mechanism. Examples of these would be the Resource Discovery Network (RDN) [http://www.rdn.ac.uk] or the Social Sciences

Information Gateway (SOSIG) [http://www.sosig.ac.uk]. If you search for psychology information via the RDN you will find yourself using SOSIG information, as the RDN is built up partly from an amalgamation of many more specific databases. Another valuable part of the RDN is the 'Virtual Training Suites', which provide you with introductions to information searching skills specific to particular academic disciplines. You will find the 'Internet Psychologist' pages at http://www.vts. rdn.ac.uk/tutorial/psychologist.

Look briefly at the Web addresses given above. These are sometimes referred to as URLs (Unique Resource Locators). These addresses are of a standard form, which you needn't worry about (unless you are interested), but the bit to look out for is the '.ac.uk' part. This indicates that the address belongs to the United Kingdom academic community and, as such, might be more reliable for academic purposes than an address located in the '.co.uk' or '.com' domains. Academic systems in the USA use the '.edu' address (for example, http://www-psych.stanford.edu), while many other countries use '.edu' followed by an indication of the country of origin (for example, http://www.psychology.uwa.edu.au). The form of the URL of a particular site is a clue that you can use to judge the reliability of the information that the page contains.

It is difficult to recommend specific Websites; it is in the nature of the Web to change and evolve, and it would be inappropriate for us to distract you from the timely and specific recommendations that will be made by your teachers. But we do want to mention Wikipedia [http://en.wikipedia.org]. This has been described as 'the best encyclopaedia in the world' and is being updated and added to on a continuous basis. You will find it an invaluable source of information on random topics. It is being maintained and created by volunteers; self-appointed experts in their fields. The nature of the Web, however, means that the contents of Wikipedia are under constant review, criticism and amendment. It is a fascinating example of the 'gift economy' of the Information Age. Remember, however, that like so much information on the Web, Wikipedia lacks the oversight of formal editorial control, and so you should always check your sources against other sources. But this is good advice when using any reference work.

WRITING WITH A WORD PROCESSOR

Most courses will now expect, if not demand, that your written work be submitted in typewritten form, and for almost everyone this will involve the use of a word processor. For some, this will mean using the computer to turn an existing handwritten final draft into a printed document. Increasingly, however, students are coming to compose their work at the keyboard, and are thereby gaining a number of significant benefits.

Dyslexia is increasingly being recognised as a common problem among students. Many people can communicate much more freely when they speak than when they write, because they are anxious that poor spelling and grammar will let them down. A spellchecker can be a great source of reassurance for those of us anxious about our spelling (see Chapter 12). The tools provided by the word processor can also make the formatting and organisation of our writing clearer, which helps the reader. This can be particularly important in longer pieces of writing where the numbering of pages and sections can make it easier for a tutor to provide specific feedback on particular points. Most importantly, perhaps, is that writing with a computer makes it easier to change and redraft what you have composed.

Closely allied to the business of writing is the collection of references to published work in books and academic journals upon which your studies and writing are based. As you progress through an undergraduate programme in psychology, you will amass a considerable list of references which you will want to be able to keep track of, and a bibliographic database will greatly assist in doing this. Your institution will have a preferred tool, or list of preferred tools. Not only will this software help you to manage and collect bibliographic references, but it will also automate the process of incorporating these references into your writing.

COMPUTER-MEDIATED COMMUNICATIONS

Electronic mail (e-mail) is an excellent way for you to contact your lecturers, tutors and student colleagues, and for them to contact you. Most universities will provide you with an e-mail account, and will want you to use this for work-related purposes, rather than another address that you may already be using. You may choose to keep your academic communications separate from your private e-mail, or have one account forward messages to the other. Whatever you do, however, routinely read the e-mail directed to the account provided by your institution. This is where communications from your courses, tutors and other parts of the university will come, and to fail to read and respond to these will cause problems, and make you look less than organised.

Some lecturers may give an e-mail address to the class and invite them to send any questions about the lecture content to that address. With increasingly large classes and pressure of time, it may be difficult to ask questions during or at the end of lectures. Other lecturers may discourage (indeed, may explicitly forbid) questions to an e-mail address, preferring rather to invite students to post any questions on a Web-based 'discussion forum', where answers and comments can also be posted. The advantage of this approach is that a good question need then be answered only once for all to see. If you have a good question after a lecture class, you can be sure that many other people will have had a similar query. Some people find it easier to ask questions in this way than putting up a hand in class. Indeed, such online discussion systems can sometimes allow questions and comments to be posted anonymously to encourage participation (although the manager of the system will always be able to track the origin of any post, so that discourteous or inappropriate behaviour can be dealt with).

A logical extension of the use of online message forums is to broaden participation from the asking of questions to the 'discussion' of topics, allowing the class group to expand upon and explore the issues raised in a lecture. Participation in this way is something that many students are unfamiliar with, and which takes a bit of getting used to. The potential to benefit from one another's understanding through this medium is very great, although some people feel rather exposed when they express their ideas in such a public way. If such opportunities exist on your courses, however, we urge you to take them – join in and learn together so that everyone benefits. Here are some suggestions about contributing to an online discussion forum:

- Be prepared to start the ball rolling by posting your questions and comments. If you have a question, rest assured that others will appreciate your efforts in formulating and asking it.

- Make your contributions 'open' rather than 'closed' – that is, write in a way that invites your colleagues to respond to what you have said.

- Be provocative without being offensive.

- Be sensitive to the feelings of others as you respond to their postings. 'That is a really interesting point, but I feel that you perhaps miss . . .' is better than 'You completely fail to understand that . . .'![1]

- Make it clear in your posting what issue you are addressing. The system may help you to do this by grouping messages on the same topic together (sometimes referred to as a 'thread'). If it does not, use constructions like 'Following from Anne's point about the resistance to attitude change, what about the evidence that . . . ?'

- Keep your postings short and concise, and keep the discussion going. Resist the temptation to post what sounds like 'the last word' on an issue.

[1] It is interesting to reflect that a form of expression that uses qualifications and 'hedges' is more characteristic of women's spoken and online language, while an authoritative and confrontational style is more typical of men. Studies have shown that, even in systems that allow anonymous posting, judges can guess the gender of the 'speaker' with success better than chance.

Above all, be sensitive to the feelings of your readers as you write online, particularly those to whom your posting may be read as a direct response. The social psychology of computer-mediated communication is an important and expanding field. From studies in this area we know that it is easy to cause misunderstandings and for conflicts to escalate in a communicative situation where we cannot look the other person in the eye, or even hear their tone of voice. What we intend as a joke may be taken literally; other problems may occur if we fail to realise that a misunderstanding has taken place. This emphasises the importance of nonverbal feedback in normal social interactions.

An important aspect of certain sorts of computer-mediated communications (CMC) is the fact that they are 'asynchronous'. That is, contributors can be distanced from one another in time as well as space. Even when students can not synchronise their time to meet together for a face-to-face ('f2f') conversation, they can post messages to a discussion system which can then be read by others when the opportunity later arises. The asynchronous discussion can be a positive experience for those who find it difficult to muster their ideas quickly in a round-table tutorial setting. In an online discussion, you can take as much time as you need to formulate a clear statement of your idea or question before you post it for others to read.

As we write this, we are conscious that many of you will be very familiar with electronic communications from your own personal social practices. Like everything else about adapting to university, you should feel free to import your previous experiences of informal learning, while being conscious of the new conventions of higher education.

COMPUTER-BASED ASSESSMENT

Computers may be used to administer examinations and quizzes to assess your learning. These can range from relatively simple multiple-choice questions (MCQs) to more complex problem-solving tasks based on pictures or calculations. These may be used for examinations counting towards course grades, although computer-based assessment can be particularly useful for self-test formative assessment, to allow you to judge your own progress and help you direct your study efforts to those areas that the assessment suggests you are less clear about. The great thing about computer-based self-testing is that you are in control, and only you need to know how you are doing. You can take a test when you feel ready, or repeat a test again and again until you feel you have mastered a topic. Also, good formative assessment packages will provide you with feedback based on the nature of your mistakes, helping you towards developing a better understanding. If your course offers such opportunities, use them.

VIRTUAL LEARNING ENVIRONMENTS

A Virtual Learning Environment (or VLE) is a Web-based system that you may find used by your courses to bring together many of the resources and activities which we have talked about already. At its most basic, a VLE is a website that you log onto giving a user name and password, which helps you to 'navigate' around an array of important Web addresses that your teachers want you to use. The VLE may contain, or point to, readings relevant to the course or administrative information about the course and university, as well as being a forum where you can ask questions, engage in online discussions or submit your 'written' work directly for assessment rather than printing it out. It may also contain online self-assessment quizzes for you to use.

The metaphor of the 'environment' is intended to suggest a 'spatial' model of the system – that the VLE is a 'place' where you can go to engage in work-related tasks, access learning resources and communicate with your teachers and student colleagues. An important aspect of this spatial metaphor is the notion of 'virtual presence' – the feeling that you are working in direct contact with your wider circle of friends and colleagues. Some courses will work very hard to cultivate this feeling of collegiality online by encouraging informal social communications as well as work-related discussion, and by encouraging students to build their own 'home page', including images and information which convey something personal about themselves. Again, make every effort to participate in such initiatives. As psychologists, we can view these as interesting experiments in the social presentation of identity in the 'virtual world'.

STUDENTS' OWN COMPUTERS

In our own institution, for example, upwards of 70 per cent of newly arriving first year students already have their own computers, with the majority of the rest claiming plans to buy. It has almost become the case that not having a computer of one's own is a lifestyle choice. This is fine, as any higher education institution will provide ample access for students who want to work on campus with institutional equipment. Depending on your course, you may also need specialised or particularly powerful equipment that the institution will provide.

It is difficult to advise on the ownership of your own equipment, as this depends on the local environment in which you are working and will, of course, be a matter of personal priorities as to how you spend your money. There is a picture that can be painted, however, which may represent the near future for some students and institutions, and the current state of affairs for others. Your laptop computer is a personal media centre, carrying all of your music as well as the thousands of photographs you have collected with your digital camera. It will play DVDs in your recreational time, on a screen big enough for one or two people to view. All your work tools, such as word processor, statistical software and bibliographic databases are on the machine, set up just the way you want to use them, along with all the documents on which you are currently working (and have ever produced). The machine has wireless network capacity, and many areas of the campus are wireless 'hot-spots' so that you can pause between classes to read your e-mail or check some Web references. Indeed, some of your teachers will encourage you to use your laptop for note-taking in class settings. Even when you are away from a network, the laptop will carry a large collection of papers and book chapters (even whole books), downloaded from your institution's library, upon which you can work. You keep your diary, both social and study, on your machine, along with the contact information for your circle of friends and colleagues. And you never forget to make regular backup copies of all your files! Some variant of this vision is likely to be the experience of an increasing proportion of students in the near future.

RESOURCES

In this book we have made a point of referring you to resources that you can readily access online from the website of the British Psychological Society (BPS) [http://www.bps.org.uk]. In addition to these specific references, you should browse around the BPS site for other academic and career-related information. We know that you will find this site to be useful, and we hope that exploring it in this way will encourage you to look to the Web when other needs and questions arise in your work and studies.

CONCLUSION

There is no doubt that ICT has changed and will continue to change our lives, both personal and professional. The impact on university life has been significant in recent years, and the developments will continue. As psychologists we can benefit from these developments as they influence our study and research practices, but also take a substantive professional interest in the ways in which technologies influence intellectual and social practices.

FURTHER READING

Clark, A. (2003), *Natural-Born Cyborgs: Minds, Technologies and the Future of Human Intelligence*. Oxford: Oxford University Press.
Clark presents the notion that humans are naturally inclined to be users of tools, and that we are forming close cognitive and emotional links with our new technologies.

Johnson, S. (2005), *Everything Bad is Good for You: How Today's Popular Culture is Actually Making Us Smarter*, New York, London: Riverhead Books.
Far from having negative effects on human intelligence, Johnson proposes that the basis of the gradually increasing performance on intelligence tests (remember the Flynn Effect mentioned in Chapter 9?) is those very media technologies, like television and video games, often blamed for the 'dumbing down' of society.

Rheingold, H. (2003), *Smart Mobs: The Next Social Revolution*, Cambridge, MA: Perseus Publishing.
This book discusses the communication technologies such as mobile phones, text messaging and the internet which are changing the ways in which we relate to each other and conduct our social lives.

The Psychologist (1998), Special issue on teaching in the 21st Century, vol. 11, August, pp. 371–90.
Christine Howe, who edits this special issue, writes that the potential currently exists to deliver psychology degree courses using computer networks. It would be possible for students to present themselves to virtual administration suites for purposes of registration, to sit in virtual lecture theatres for multimedia teaching and to visit virtual libraries to

obtain follow-up materials. Should the students find the pressure too great, they would be able to chat to others in virtual cafes, and they would of course sit their final examinations in virtual assessment halls. A nightmare scenario perhaps! There are number of lively articles here which extol the possibilities of online learning while adding substantial cautionary notes.

14 PREPARING FOR AND SITTING EXAMINATIONS

You will already have plenty of experience in sitting exams! However, whereas at school you received a great deal of coaching and preparation for these exams, this is not the case at university. It is a good example of the difference in approach between secondary and tertiary education. This is probably as good a place as any to stress that although university teaching staff would like to see their students do well in examinations, they are invariably pursuing a full and demanding research career in addition to teaching and simply do not have as much time as they might like to deal with students' learning difficulties. So do not expect to receive the same degree of support that you experienced at school, as performance in examinations is seen as very much up to the student.

At this point it is worthwhile asking what are examinations designed to find out. They are certainly testing your knowledge about the subjects you have studied, but more importantly are an opportunity for students to demonstrate their understanding of the subject and how far they can think critically and creatively about what they have read. You will have become used to the idea of a particular textbook in connection with schoolwork and this is likely to also be true of first year university courses. But you may well find that you are issued with a reading list containing several books and, even in first year, some articles from academic journals. Getting used to consulting several sources from the very start of your course is a good strategy, as you will encounter slightly different perspectives if not outright disagreement on some topics. Demonstrating your awareness that there may be more than one view of a theory or interpretation of an experiment makes you think about why this should be, and in so doing aids your own understanding of the problem and helps you then to write more clearly about it.

It should be obvious by now that preparing for exams starts with developing good study skills (see Chapter 10) and work habits. This creates in the memory a body of knowledge into which new facts can be incorporated and new links made to existing knowledge (see Chapter 6). With this in place, the examination is no longer such a daunting prospect. It is then possible for the well-prepared individual to achieve the lateral thinking and creativity which mark out the first class student.

Make sure that you are familiar with the kind of exam set in your course – there will be copies of previous papers available in the library or on websites supporting the course. You will find there are questions covering the whole of the course, which very often means that you can focus on those aspects that you found most interesting and be certain of getting questions in that area. Does this mean we are in favour of question-spotting? No, if it means neglecting certain areas of the course, but in reality many students will do this, perhaps because of time constraints and the demands of work in other subjects of their degree. Familiarity with the form of questions and the realisation that there is a certain reliability of topic areas will do a great deal to reduce your anxiety.

The first task in sitting down at your exam desk should be to read the paper carefully and think which three or four questions you will choose from the dozen or so on offer. *This is very difficult to do.* You will be surrounded by large numbers of your peers, most of whom will be avidly writing away before you have even read to the end of the exam paper, and the pressure to join them is very strong. It is quality not quantity that the examiners want to see, however, and a well-written and tightly argued page and a half may be worth far more than half a dozen pages of unstructured and ill-thought-out regurgitation of lecture notes. Indeed, if you put yourself in the examiners' shoes, the piece of work which stands out is the one that is different to the others, so spending some time in thinking about the best way to write your answer, and perhaps doing this in a way which does not slavishly follow the lecture material, can pay dividends.

DIFFERENT FORMS OF QUESTION

In introductory classes you can often exempt yourself from final year exams by achieving above a certain mark in your coursework. This has the drawback that you may postpone taking exams until a stage in your university career where performance counts towards your final degree class, and inexperience with exams then becomes more daunting. A less threatening form of exam assessment is the multiple choice format, where you are asked to select the correct answer from four possible answers to a question. This is easier in the sense that one stage of the retrieval process from memory has been done for you by the question setter – you are only required to recognise the correct answer from an array. Because multiple choice relies strongly on recognition memory, which is easier than recall tasks, performance is generally better. Of course, to recognise the correct answer, the information has to be available in memory – nothing can bypass this stage of acquisition! Multiple choice exams are also designed to penalise the random guesser, so incorrect selection carries an additional penalty. Here are some typical examples:

1. Bill is a young boy and he knows that fish swim and birds fly. At the zoo he sees a penguin swimming under the water and says to his Mum, 'Look, the black and white fish is swimming.' This is an illustration of:
   a) the process of accommodation

   b) the process of assimilation

   c) egocentric thinking

   d) inability to understand the principle of object permanence

2. You are looking at a very blurry photograph. At first all you see is a vague red circle, but after looking at the picture for a minute or so, you finally realise this is an orange. You have moved from:

a) perception to adaptation

b) perception to sensation

c) sensation to perception

d) sensation to synaesthesia

It is very common to find this kind of question at the end of chapters in introductory textbooks as an aid to helping you see how much you have understood. Even these two examples should help convince you that this form of assessment can be very effective. The advantage this has for the assessor is that the exam can be administered in a computer format, or at least scored using a computer, and moreover – if correctly designed – is completely objective since there is only one correct answer in each instance.

The most common form of exam question requires you to write an essay, or perhaps to write short notes on a topic. For example:

1. Give an account of the structure of human memory.

2. Write short notes on FOUR of the following: patient H. M.; LTM; STM; mnemonics; hippocampus; recency effect; eyewitness testimony; cognitive interview.

These two questions cover the same material, but if you elect to answer the second question you must make sure that you attempt *all* four components, as each carries equal marks. Failure to attempt one component will automatically lose a quarter of the marks for that question. Many students make this mistake, producing good B grade or 2:1 standard answers for each of the three components, only to end up with an overall C grade for the question because they failed to attempt the fourth part.

As you are trying to convince the examiners that you are on top of the material, don't be afraid to use diagrams and illustrations in your answer. Psychology is a scientific subject, and it is entirely appropriate to reproduce figures or outlines of models in your answer. A good diagram can often convey far more relevant information than the same half page of text. Try to aim for an answer in which you are making four or five substantive points – it is these points that you should list in any essay plan you outline prior to answering the question proper. In recent years we have noticed a tendency to overextend the plan which students include in their exam answers. If you find plans helpful, then by all means include them, but they are not obligatory. What is most important is that your answer is pertinent and focused. Indeed, a useful byproduct of the more considered essay is that handwriting is improved because you are not writing pages of script at a high speed. Again, think about the problems the marker faces: legibility is of the essence, and your handwriting will be better if you write less.

All universities provide students with details of how their work is assessed, and these marking scales are a very clear guide to what the examiners are looking for. We reproduce one such below – the fine detail will vary between institutions, but there will be a broad agreement. What differences exist, however, explains why universities have external examiners in addition to the lecturers who teach a particular course. It is the job of external examiners from another university to see that standards are assured and degree classes comparable across institutions.

All universities award honours degrees in which the quality of the degree is stratified into broad bands of classification. The kind of honours degree obtained is used by employers and selection boards to mark a particular threshold for applicants. If you look at the job advertisements in national newspapers such as *the Times, the Guardian, the Telegraph* and *the Independent* you will see that a 2:1 degree is often required as entry for postgraduate courses. This is very likely to be the case for postgraduate training in psychology, so if you want to continue into a professional career as a clinical, educational or occupational psychologist, you should aim for a good upper second class honours degree.

MARKING SCALE AND EXAM GRADE DESCRIPTORS

Grade

A **70–100 per cent FIRST** Direct answer; coherent argument supported by appropriate evidence. Understanding and evaluation of both theory and method. Evidence of extensive reading and of independent thinking. *Better candidates (75+) also do some/all of: bring in cross-disciplinary links, challenge key assumptions, offer novel interpretations.*

B **60–69 per cent UPPER SECOND** Direct answer; coherent argument supported by appropriate evidence. Accurate in citing theory, well informed, no major omissions. *Better candidates also show evidence of wide reading, capacity to evaluate and a good balance of evaluation and description. A mark of 65 or above should only be awarded if there are indications that the answer goes beyond lecture coverage by showing evidence of additional reading and/or independent evaluation of the material.*

C **50–59 per cent LOWER SECOND** Answers majority of the question. Answer is descriptive rather than evaluative and may have some minor factual omissions. Lacks a fully coherent argument; cites evidence but not always appropriately. *Better candidates attempt to construct an argument, have no factual omissions and attempt to evaluate.*

D **40–49 per cent THIRD** Does not fully answer the question; may miss point of question / include irrelevant material, lacks coherence. Major omissions of fact. Seeks to evaluate but inappropriately. *Better candidates construct an answer that tells an appropriate story, achieve a degree of factual accuracy and try to cite evidence.*

E **35–39 per cent MARGINAL FAIL** A poor quality answer which narrowly avoids the 'clear fail' category because the marker decides there is evidence of sufficient knowledge to show a general familiarity with the subject matter. It will have two or more of the following features:

very limited knowledge
omits material of major importance
fails to answer part of the question

much too brief

contains misinformation

contains irrelevant material

has incoherent or confused statements

F *25–34 per cent CLEAR FAIL* This grade indicates insufficient evidence of serious academic study. The answer fails for one or more reasons:

fails to demonstrate knowledge or understanding

has basic misunderstandings

incoherent

all or much of the material is irrelevant to the question

G *0–24 per cent BAD FAIL* Upper end, a few superficial points made; lower end, no answer (0) or perhaps one or two sentences of relevance.

REVISION STRATEGIES

We have emphasised already that good study techniques repay themselves in making revising for exams much less of a slog. You should basically understand the material covered in the course and your task now is to remember this and, wherever possible, make links both with other areas of psychology and outside the discipline. If you look at the exam grade descriptors above, you will see this is an essential requirement for the very best answers.

Make sure that you start revising for the exam in plenty of time. Ideally, try some revision sessions with friends in which you get one another to explain key concepts or attempt outline answers to questions. If you can explain something well to a friend or to someone who has not taken the course, and they find your account interesting, you will be able to write well about this topic in the exam. If you are prone to anxiety attacks and panic before or during exams, then discuss your problem with someone in the university learning support team. They will have encountered every conceivable problem in the past and may offer courses on coping with exams. This is true of many other aspects of life at university

– there will be workshops on essay writing, creative thinking, preparing for dissertations and so on. It is the rare student who will not gain by attending some sessions of this kind, and we would urge you to take advantage of what your institution offers.

FURTHER READING

Leman, P. (2004), 'And your chosen specialist subject is . . .', *The Psychologist*, vol. 17, April, pp. 196–8.
Patrick Leman is at Royal Holloway College in the University of London. He examines the disparities in awarding first class degrees in different subjects, asking why men seem to out-number women in achieving that elusive first. Is it because men are more likely to take risks in their writing and produce work which is seen to be more original, controversial and therefore 'first class'?

Newstead, S. (2004), 'Time to make our mark', *The Psychologist*, vol. 17, January, pp. 20–3.
Professor Newstead of Plymouth University has published many articles on the examining process. Here he looks at issues of assessment from the viewpoint of the teacher, and argues that psychology can improve the reliability and validity of student assessment.

INDEX